A playbook for
that matter to

BEYOND SIZZLE

THE NEXT EVOLUTION OF BRANDING

BY MONA AMODEO

Robin,

In Gratitude for and
some Inspiration to matter
Commitment to making
The World Better!

Mona
Dec 2018

MAVEN HOUSE

Maven House Press
4 Snead Ct., Palmyra, VA 22963
Find us on the web at www.mavenhousepress.com

Cover Design by Kristoffer Poore • Layout Designed by Somi Choi
idgroup, a brand transformation firm. Pensacola, FL
www.idgroupbranding.com

Library of Congress Control Number: 9781938548154

Paperback ISBN: 978-1-938548-15-4

Printed in the United States of America

If you are an entrepreneurial thinker ready to embrace the opportunity to prosper economically by having a positive impact on people, communities, and the world; a game changer courageous enough to challenge the status quo by designing and leading organizations as brands that matter; or a leader who wants to make choices that leave the world better than you found it, keep reading.

"EDUCATING THE MIND WITHOUT EDUCATING THE HEART
IS NO EDUCATION AT ALL."

— ARISTOTLE

PART II

THE BRANDING FROM THE CORE® PLAYBOOK

PREFACE

Dear Reader,

Thank you for joining me on this journey to the Next Evolution of Branding. This book is about branding, but not branding as you most likely think of it. As you read the following pages, some of the ideas may feel familiar to you. However, this book offers a bold perspective that branding reimagined, has the power to build more productive, more innovative, and more purposeful organizations that not only thrive economically, but also have a positive impact on customers, employees, and the world.

My *idgroup* colleagues and I evolved this approach to branding over the past 15 years as we've worked with organizations of all shapes and sizes, from start-ups to global corporations, as well as not-for-profits and public entities. We coined this methodology, *Branding from the Core*. Why that name? Because this is about shaping meaning that emanates from the core of an organization: who it is, what it believes and what it wants to share with the world. Reaching beyond the spin often associated with advertising and marketing-focused initiatives, this fresh new view of branding aims to engage the voices of the organization in shaping, sharing, and living its unique and authentic story. The result is two-fold: an engaged team of employees who are moving together toward a shared vision, and the creation of a brand people trust. We describe it as branding that reaches beyond sizzle to substance.

This view builds the ethical business case for transforming organizations into *brands that matter*, and integrates corporate responsibility with best practices from the fields of organization development, change management, communications, and marketing. This book repositions branding not as a departmental initiative or a campaign, but as an approach to managing the whole organization, specifically the *interactions within and between the organization and its environment.*

Branding from the Core was developed with one foot in the world of research and the other in the "real" world of business. I approached the writing of this book in the same manner. Solutions offered on the following pages are anchored in the rigors of research—my own and that of some really smart people that I have had the opportunity to work with and learn from over the years. The knowledge gained from this research—combined with my own experiences working with clients—produced the perspectives shared in this book.

I hope you'll find the information presented here to be thought-provoking, inspirational, and most importantly, practical. I open the book with "My Inspiration," which provides the backstory of my branding philosophy. This experience rekindled my belief in the power of leaders and organizations to be a positive force in the world and redirected my career path to helping others embrace their power to move *business-as-is* to *business as-it-can-be.*

In the words of Peter Drucker, father of modern management, "If you want to predict the future, create it." I hope this book inspires you to do just that. As a corollary, I find the cautionary words of Thomas Edison equally important: "Vision without execution is just hallucination." While I believe the words on these pages will encourage you to think big, I also hope that the practical playbook outlined in second part of the book will engage your stakeholders, ignite purpose, unify their voices, and as a result, elevate and amplify the influence of your organization as a brand that matters—to customers, employees, and the world.

Trust the process. Enjoy the journey.

Mona,
Gulf Breeze, Florida
June 1, 2018

IF YOU WANT TO PREDICT THE FUTURE, CREATE IT.

PETER DRUCKER

"I don't think any CEO expects to stand before his maker someday talking about shareholder value that he created. A corporation makes a profit to exist. It's not the other way around. It's not existing to make a profit. In my view, it ought to exist for some higher purpose than just shareholder value. And that higher purpose extends to responsibility for all creation."

Ray C. Anderson (1934–2011)
Founder, Interface, Inc.

MY INSPIRATION:
THE INTERFACE BACKSTORY

In the words of the Greek philosopher Heraclitus, "No man ever steps in the same river twice, for it's not the same river and he's not the same man." The people we meet and the experiences we have along life's path change us. Some more than others. The opportunity to conduct a research project with global carpet manufacturer and sustainability pioneer **Interface, Inc.,**˙ awakened me to what's possible when people are fully engaged in working for something they believe in and feel connected to.

During the course of this research, I experienced firsthand the capacity of purpose to ignite the passions of people. An excerpt from one of the many interviews I conducted with the company's employees demonstrates this point:

> When I am lying on my deathbed and someone asks what I did with my life, who cares if I say I, we, produced thousands of rolls of really great carpet, but if I can say that I was a part of something that changed the business models so we are working with the environment and not against it—creating a better world for our children and their children—now that's saying something.

Billy, *Interface engineer, 2004*

˙*Interface, Inc.* is the world's largest manufacturer of modular carpet. The company produces the carpet squares you have likely seen in commercial buildings, or even in someone's home.

THE STORY

This story begins in Atlanta, Georgia, in March 2004, with my introduction to the man who would become known as the "radical industrialist." That man was Ray C. Anderson (1934–2011), the founder of Interface, Inc. Thinking back to that first encounter with Ray, I remember being very excited to have finally landed a meeting that I had worked for months to secure. As I stepped off the elevator at Overlook, Interface's corporate headquarters in Atlanta, I had no idea that step would be the first in a journey that would reshape many of the views I held about business, and about the direction of my career. Over the years Ray became a teacher, mentor, and friend that I feel honored to have known.

I first became aware of Interface and Ray through an article given to me by a colleague in my doctoral program. He was aware of my growing interest in **sustainable business**˙ as a research topic for my dissertation and thought Interface might be worth exploring. The article spoke of how Anderson, a Georgia Tech-educated industrial engineer and entrepreneur, was transforming his company from what he described as a "plunderer of the earth" to an exemplar of sustainable manufacturing. As I read the article, I became interested, although more than a little skeptical.

While the early sustainability pioneers (exemplified by names like Ben & Jerry's, The Body Shop, and Tom's of Maine)

˙*Sustainability* is most often defined as meeting the needs of the present without compromising the ability of future generations to meet theirs. There are three main pillars: social, environmental, and economic. These three pillars are informally referred to as people, planet, and profits.

had inspired my interest in the emerging **triple bottom line concept of business,*** they also led me to ask a different question. These early adopters were founded with the values of social and environmental responsibility infused in their culture, but I wondered if a company *not* born with this DNA could change. Interface looked like the perfect place to find the answers.

Having grown up in Georgia in the heart of the southern textile world, I understood a little about the traditional mindset of manufacturers. I was pretty sure that neither the word *sustainability* nor the concept *triple bottom line accounting* championed by Interface was a part of this industry's vocabulary. Yet here was a profitable and successful carpet manufacturer being lauded by leading environmentalists as a hero. Several questions came to mind: Was this the real deal, or just PR spin? And if it *was* real, how did this transformation happen? These questions became the focus of my research.

For more than a year, I lived and breathed Interface. Ray and his team gave me full access to the people who had been a part of the journey. I listened to stories from the corner office to the shop floor. Forty interviews, mounds of archival data, and yards of video footage captured hours of conversations with Ray and others and led to a 250-page document—my dissertation—"Becoming Sustainable: Identity Dynamics Within

---

**Triple bottom line* is an accounting framework that was coined by entrepreneur and corporate responsibility expert John Elkington in 1994. It takes a broader view of measuring performance beyond the traditional single bottom line: profits. The model includes social, environmental, and economic performance metrics (JohnElkington.com).

Transformational Culture Change at Interface" (a title only an academic can produce). But, as esoteric as it sounds, this title does capture the essence of what was learned.

RAY ANDERSON'S VISION FOR INTERFACE

"to be the first company that, by its deeds, shows the entire industrial world what sustainability is in all its dimensions: people, process, product, place, and profits—by 2020— and in doing so we will become restorative through the power of influence." (August 1994)

Over the span of my research, as employee after employee shared their stories, it became increasingly clear that Interface was able to transform itself because its people became connected to a deeper purpose for their work, more than simply making great carpet. Anderson created this connection by engaging them as central players in bringing his vision to life. Maybe his days playing football for Bobby Dodd at Georgia Tech embedded his understanding of the unstoppable energy of a fired-up team united by a shared vision of doing something really big.

The stories shared by the people who were a part of the Interface journey to sustainability reflected a transformation of their attitudes from skepticism to commitment as they embraced the need to take responsibility for the negative impact their company was having on the environment—and do something about it (Amodeo, 2008). One of the marketing executives said it this way, "I don't come to work every day just to sell another yard of carpet that people walk on, or wipe their feet on, or that makes their office more beautiful. I am here to build a better world for us and for our grandchildren. We know there's a better way, and we're here to prove it." *Better* for them translated into proving that building great products and a profitable business could sit side by side with leaving a better world for future generations.

A petroleum-intensive carpet company becoming a symbol of environmental stewardship? Imagine just how unattainable that seemed to the people of Interface in 1994.

Yet I learned from Interface and subsequent clients to never underestimate people's ability to achieve a seemingly impossible dream when they're committed to a purpose.

Nonetheless, embracing change didn't happen overnight. One of the company's first employees summed up the reaction most had when they first heard Ray's challenge: "To be honest, we thought he'd [Anderson] gone 'round the bend. We kept thinking that it would just go away, but it didn't; he just kept at it."

The same pioneering spirit and tenacity that had driven Ray Anderson to introduce the "crazy" idea of carpet tiles, which birthed the company in 1973, had once again led him to go beyond the limits of "the way we've always done things." His entrepreneurial spirit and commitment to a new set of values set Interface on a new course. Unwavering focus ultimately infused an entire company with a heightened sense of purpose, enthusiasm, and determination to prove that he and they were right. New behaviors associated with this vision fundamentally reshaped how the people of Interface redefined the purpose of their company as they moved over the years from initial skepticism to advocates for Anderson's views. Over a four-year period, Interface emerged with a new brand as a leader and an authentic symbol of a new, more-sustainable approach to manufacturing. It had rejected the false choice between profit or responsibility, and it was proving that it was possible to produce innovative products that people wanted, be profitable, *and* take care of the environment. These efforts were reinforced with rounds of applause from people both inside and outside of the organization. People wanted to be a part of this company that was changing the face of manufacturing.

THE POWER OF PURPOSE

Answers to *how* others can transform their organizations into a brand that matters, just as Interface did, emerged from one of the most important insights I learned from Ray Anderson and the people of Interface during my time studying and consulting with the company.

> *Great organization brands are anchored in the connections people feel to a vision that is meaningful to them. Their engagement with a collective purpose creates levels of performance that cannot be forged by surface-level attempts to motivate people.*

PURPOSE MATTERS. It feeds the soul and replenishes our energy. Purpose lived through actions anchors us, connects us, motivates us, and ultimately defines us. Life fueled by the search for our own personal *why* is the very definition of the human spirit. Today, we all seem to be searching more than ever for human connections that support our life's journey. The illusory promises offered by technology, in a strange way, have done just the opposite. Tweets aren't conversation, and Facebook "likes" don't define relationships. This vacuum created by these promises has been intensified by the speed of change, which has spun us into thousands of disconnected pieces and parts, often leaving us wondering where we belong, and if anything we do really matters.

So, what does all of this have to do with *Beyond Sizzle: The Next Evolution of Branding*, a book you most likely found in the business section of your favorite bookstore? While the impact of purpose and the importance of relationships can't be directly accounted for in a spreadsheet or an accountant's ROI calculation, both purpose and relationships influence, in so many ways, everything that ultimately defines the traditional bottom-line measurements of success.

A confluence of forces is fueling the awakening of leaders to the potential of organizations to reach new levels of prosperity by becoming places where employees are more engaged, excited, and productive because they feel that what they do has an impact beyond the moment, the year, or even their lifetimes. They matter.

This truth is being reinforced with increasing frequency by researchers, authors, and other thought leaders—all proclaiming the growing influence of corporate purpose and values alignment on decisions about whom we choose to work for, purchase from, or contribute to.

Old ideas that limit the purpose of business to quarterly shareholder returns are being toppled. People are rewarding companies who have an expanded view of success measured by the triple bottom line. It's clear. This once-fringe business perspective often associated with Birkenstocks and granola, now has a seat at the boardroom table. There is much for all of us to learn from Interface and from others who have blazed new paths to prosperity fueled by purpose.

Can organizations matter more because they become places where people live their values, where ideas are nurtured, grow, and thrive? Can they become environments where people feel excited and engaged in being a part of producing innovations that make their communities and the world, better? Can they become a force for change? How can we correct a trajectory that by our own hands has produced real

THIS IS NOT ONLY THE RIGHT THING TO DO, IT'S THE SMART THING TO DO.

threats to the quality of our lives and the legacy we leave future generations? And, can this type of company create positive energy that radiates beyond its walls to attract and retain the trust and loyalty of customers, donors, or investors?

Absolutely. It has been done by some.
Therefore, it can be done by many.

The Interface research answered my original question about if and how a company, not born with the DNA of sustainability values, could change its culture. But my search for these answers also spawned new insights into the connections between culture change and branding. Over the past fifteen years, my exploration of this connection has led to the insights in this book about what it takes to transform organizations into brands that matter to customers, employees, and the world—just as Interface did.

Today, the world is searching for more companies like Interface. By this I mean companies that embrace the importance of corporate responsibility demonstrated in both words and actions. I hope this book will support leaders who are ready to respond to this call. In the words of Ray Anderson, "This is not only the right thing to do, it's the smart thing to do, from a pure business perspective."

PART I BEGINS HERE

PART I
BUILDING ON THE
SHOULDERS OF GIANTS

BUILDING ON THE SHOULDERS OF GIANTS

"Everybody talks about 'find your purpose, find your purpose, find your purpose'—the truth is we all have the same purpose. And we should all quit looking. Our purpose is to serve humanity."   — Tim Cook, Apple CEO

While my sixties soul may have motivated the search for the answers shared on these pages, *The Next Evolution of Branding* reaches beyond the ethical case, to the business case, for why now is the time for organizations of all sizes to seize the opportunity to become *brands that matter*. This is not about spin or some philosophical, starry-eyed kind of vision, nor is it about bolted-on commitment. Rather, it's about helping organizations compete more effectively by rallying people around a shared purpose. While many have talked about why this connection is of growing importance to the success of companies, *The Next Evolution of Branding* bridges the execution gap by translating this philosophy into action through the Branding from the Core® process introduced in Part II of this book.

The chapters in Part I of this book introduce the foundational ideas upon which *The Next Evolution of Branding* stands. In Part II, titled the Playbook, these ideas are brought to life through Branding from the Core, as a process that reaches beyond platitudes and philosophy to transform organizations into brands that matter, even if they don't have a Ray Anderson. The answers to what it means to be a *Brand that Matters* are as individual as each organization. I hope this book will guide you on a journey of figuring out what it means to your organization.

CHAPTER 1: WHY WE NEED A NEW APPROACH TO BRANDING

This chapter traces the evolution of branding and identifies challenges to approaches that rely too heavily on externally focused image development.

CHAPTER 2: A NEW PARADIGM OF BRANDING

This chapter challenges common thinking and introduces the principles that underpin *The Next Evolution of Branding*. Embracing this approach to managing *organizations as brands* will support leaders in overcoming the disruptive forces that are challenging the efforts of companies to stand out in the crowd.

CHAPTER 3: THE INVISIBLE FORCE OF BRANDING

This chapter explains identification as the invisible force that forges connections between people and brands. It also explores the growing importance of a tribe known as Cultural Creatives and the parallel growth of a business philosophy known by many names, including Conscious Capitalism, purpose-driven, and triple bottom line, and why understanding this view of business is critical to building successful organizations.

CHAPTER 4: FROM SIZZLE TO SUBSTANCE

This chapter offers the seemingly radical proposition that a profession often associated with the self-absorbed spin artists exemplified in the hit television series *Mad Men* can be a positive force in the world. We take a closer look at emerging opportunities to grow business through values-based branding, some companies who are doing it, and organizations that can support your journey to becoming a brand that matters.

....

CHAPTER 5: THE OPERATING SYSTEM OF BRANDS

It is said that culture eats strategy for lunch. This chapter explains why. The strength of a culture is often what people mean when they say that an organization is hardwired to act in a certain way. Failing to acknowledge this hardwiring is why so many change efforts fail. This chapter explains the important link between culture and transforming organizations into brands that matter.

The following are key terms that are used throughout this book.

BRAND. A brand is defined as the socially constructed meaning people associate with the name of a product, place, or person.

BRANDING. The process of managing the elements that construct the desired meaning of the brand. It is shaped by aligning the visual and verbal communications with the experiences people have with the brand.

THE NEXT EVOLUTION OF BRANDING. This new paradigm provides a set of management principles that addresses the disruptions challenging the ability of companies to build and strengthen authenticity, trust, and reputation.

BRANDS THAT MATTER. These are companies we love to love because they stand for something more than what they sell. They have earned a reputation not only for delivering quality products or services but also for being great places to work, for pushing their industries forward, and for striving to make a positive difference in the world. These companies have successfully integrated the characteristics of desirability, distinctiveness, credibility, and responsibility into the core of their brands.

BRANDING FROM THE CORE. Branding from the Core is a next evolution branding process and strategic management framework that helps leaders transform their organizations into brands that matter. This integrated methodology engages stakeholders in shaping, sharing, and living the organization's unique and authentic story.

"Would you tell me, please, which way I ought to go from here?"

— Lewis Carroll
Alice in Wonderland

CHAPTER 1:
WHY WE NEED A NEW APPROACH TO BRANDING

Who are you, and why should I care? The success of every organization depends on responding to these questions with answers compelling enough for people to choose it over the competition.

Since its inception in the 1950s, companies have relied on branding as an advertising tactic to cut through the clutter of choices by building emotional connections between the qualities of their brand and the motivations of their audiences. When done well, branding creates a competitive advantage by building relationships people trust. However, three emerging trends in today's complex marketplace have presented new challenges to influencing the choices people make about who to buy from, work for, and invest in. These shifts include: the hyperconnection of people forged by technology, the growing skepticism of the formal communications pushed out by organizations, and the shifting expectations about the responsibility of business. Successfully responding to these shifts is critical to creating the trust needed to position organizations to compete. For branding to continue to be the economic engine it has been for over seventy years, we need to answer these questions: *Can branding be used to overcome these challenges* and *What is The Next Evolution of Branding?*

A Short History

One of the biggest challenges within any discussion about branding is the multiple perspectives people bring to the conversation about what the word means. I like to compare defining branding to explaining the color *red*. Both have various shades of meaning depending on who is doing the talking. The confusion is not surprising, given how the practice of branding developed. It is important to understand this evolution and some of the key terms associated with the word brand before moving forward with our exploration of *The Next Evolution of Branding.*

While there are slightly nuanced definitions, most agree that a *brand* is defined by the meaning people associate with a company, product, person, place, or thing. This is often expressed by the phrase, "Your brand lives in the minds of others." *Branding*, on the other hand, is the process of *intentionally* creating desired meaning. The confusion in conversations about branding usually swirls around the words *brand* and *logo* being used interchangeably. While inextricably linked, a logo is not a brand and a brand is not a logo.

Logo is a shortened form of *logogram*. It originates from the Greek *logos*, which means *word*. The use of logos emerged in commerce as pictograms, or visual shorthand, that shopkeepers displayed outside their places of business, to explain services offered. This was an important method of communicating with a large number of people who, in those days, could not read. So, the logo developed simply as a symbolic identity used to guide people to products or services they were looking to purchase.

The word *brand*, on the other hand, has its roots in the practice of burning distinct symbols into the hides of livestock to show ownership. It was important for the "brand" to be unique enough to differentiate one owner's livestock from the others. The use of these unique symbols of differentiation was co-opted more broadly by business and industry with the rise of the Industrial Age.

Over time, trademark law has added legal and economic value to these symbols.

Modern trademark law reaches back in Europe to the late nineteenth century, when the Merchandise Marks Act of 1862 made it illegal to imitate another's trademark for purposes of confusing the consumer. The roots of today's trademark practices in the United States are found in the Trademark Act of 1946, also known as the Lanham Act, which protects a business's commercial identity or brand by discouraging other businesses from adopting a name or logo that is "confusingly similar" to an existing trademark.

What we know today as branding emerged at a time when advertisers were charged with driving the growth of businesses during a period when standardization of manufacturing made functional differences in quality less and less evident. As products became more commoditized, companies sought new answers about how to distinguish their goods from the competition. They needed more than unique symbols and a list of features and benefits to differentiate their products. Around the same time, the growth of mass media, in the forms of radio and television, gave advertisers more ways to reach larger numbers of people with messages about the products they were selling. The need to find new answers to how to convince customers that their products were better than the competition, together with the explosion of mass media channels, birthed what became known as The Golden Age of Advertising.

The Golden Age of Advertising

The Golden Age of Advertising was propelled by many of the ideas contained in *Propaganda*, a book written by **Edward Bernays***
(1928). It provided the lessons that Madison Avenue was looking for to give their clients a leg up. Bernays, who is considered the father of public relations, was also the nephew of Sigmund Freud. Building on his uncle's notion that irrational forces drive human behaviors, Bernays offered advertisers new ideas about how to differentiate products by combining theories of group psychology with the growing power of mass media. He argued that by triggering emotional associations between products and the aspirations of people, companies could persuade large numbers of people to change their behavior. In other words, buy their products. Bernays believed the use of what he called propaganda was valuable to commerce because it helped to reduce consumers' anxiety by cutting through the clutter of decision making:

....

*Edward Bernays (1891–1995) is considered the pioneer of public relations. His influence radically changed the persuasion tactics used in advertising and political campaigns.

> *In theory, everybody buys the best and cheapest commodities offered him on the market. In practice, if everyone went around pricing, and chemically testing before purchasing, the dozens of soaps or fabrics or brands of bread which are for sale, economic life would become hopelessly jammed. To avoid such confusion, society consents to have its choices narrowed to ideas and objects brought to its attention through propaganda of all kinds.*

By the 1960s, advertising agencies had become evangelists of Bernays's philosophies, using mass media to connect large groups of people with products and services based on perceptions of value created by emotionally charged advertising. Companies turned to these creative gurus to sell their products through engaging campaigns that featured catchy headlines and enticing visuals that tapped into people's aspirations, rather than just convincing them of the superiority of product features. This is illustrated in Coca-Cola's reframing of its 1905 selling proposition from a statement of medicinal benefits, **"Coca-Cola Revives and Sustains,"** to the emotional connections created by the 1970 campaign "I'd Like to Buy the World a Coke," which linked drinking Coca-Cola to aspirations of building a more peaceful world. Songwriter, singer, and producer Billy Davis produced the commercial, which featured a

'1905 Coa-Cola Ad positions the functional benefits of Coke as a prescription for weariness.

diverse group of young people on a hilltop singing a message of hope and inclusiveness. What became known as the Coca-Cola Hilltop campaign boosted Coke sales by tapping into the hopes of a Vietnam War-weary world. The ability to create perceptions of possibility such as this propelled the growth of the advertising industry and fueled the explosion of the consumer products industry, which in turn had tremendous economic impact.

What Has Changed?

Over the past seventy years, the methods born of the Golden Age of Advertising have evolved into what we call branding. The business has exploded into a multibillion-dollar industry responsible for building perceptions about everything from coffee to corporations. The practice includes the creation of names, visual symbols, and emotional communications aimed at *intentionally* influencing perceptions through building symbolic meaning—the emotional side of marketing responsible for tapping into feelings that sway people to choose X over Y.

One of the reasons branding has proven to be so powerful for so many years is the experts controlled the medium and the message. This stands in stark contrast to the reality faced by organizations today. The power of influence lies largely in the hands of the masses connected by technology. The interconnectedness of people, supported by the mushrooming number of communication channels, has democratized influence. This is combined with an increasingly skeptical public who put more faith in customer reviews than in the advertising and other formal communications generated by organizations. Let's face it, the masses have emerged as viral mediums of messages and attitudes, empowered to build or destroy reputations with the stroke of a key. More than ever, they are the co-creators of perception and thus important partners in the creation of brands.

Today, it isn't enough to sell just the sizzle. People want to know the company that stands behind the glitz of its product advertising. This requires organizations to set themselves, not just their products, apart from the competition and has intensified the importance of building corporate brands. A different approach to branding is needed than was used by product branders.

> **THIS REQUIRES ORGANIZATIONS TO SET THEMSELVES, NOT JUST THEIR PRODUCTS, APART FROM THE COMPETITION AND HAS INTENSIFIED THE IMPORTANCE OF BUILDING CORPORATE BRANDS.**

While both corporate branding and product branding share the goal of influencing the choices people make, branding an organization is fundamentally different from product branding. The credibility of a product brand is controlled on the assembly line and through packaging. These factors dictate the experiences people have with the product. If I open a Coca-Cola in Pensacola, Florida, my experience with that product is almost guaranteed to be consistent with a bottle of Coke I open in San Francisco, California. On the other hand, perceptions about the authenticity of an organization brand are determined by the alignment between the words and deeds of the *people* who stand behind the brand.

TODAY, IT ISN'T ENOUGH TO SELL JUST THE SIZZLE.

Creating loyalty to corporate brands is increasingly complex, requiring a focus on authenticity and transparency that is very different from what was needed to influence past generations to buy the latest and, greatest products. The following sections explore the three disruptive forces that are challenging the bonds of trust needed to create strong corporate brands.

DISRUPTIVE FORCE 1 | SKEPTICISM

Over the years, the power of persuasive messaging propelled the explosion of consumerism in America and ignited the growth of industry. While we can credit The Golden Age of Advertising for fueling economic growth and prosperity, it also had a downside. This darkside garnered advertising professionals a reputation for manipulating information as a means to convince people to do what the advertisers wanted. Many viewed them as *spinmeisters*, who often ignored facts in order to sell their wares. Even worse, in some cases they became co-conspirators of harm. Such was the case in the use of images of the macho cowboy who promised smokers that they too could become a rugged, sexy Marlboro Man with the purchase of a pack of cigarettes. These convincing campaigns continued in the face of medical evidence confirming the damaging effects of tobacco on humans. No harm there, right? While we would like to believe that companies have learned their lesson about the importance of authenticity, that doesn't appear to be the case.

According to the *2017 Edelman Trust Barometer*, 2016 to 2017 reflected the largest-ever drop in trust of media, businesses, and government: "Forty-five percent of respondents reported trust in business in 2016. That number dropped to just 33 percent in 2017." This loss of faith has resulted in the marketplace questioning the formal messaging pushed out by companies and their advertising and public relations agencies.

A recent example that has fed into the modern narrative that business can't be trusted is the backlash against Facebook for its perceived lack of transparency about the company's failure to protect information collected from its users. Another example of why the bonds of trust between people and corporations have weakened is found in the tarnishing of the long-respected reputation of Volkswagen because of revelations that the company equipped their diesel cars with software that could cheat on emissions test. Enough said. There are many more examples of deception, some more or less extreme or detrimental, but let's just agree there's a reason that people have grown distrustful and skeptical of the authenticity of messaging produced by organizations. This skepticism has been intensified further by the increased ability of people to share information and opinions via the internet and social media. The customer has become empowered, and is increasingly and constantly demanding, "PROVE IT."

DISRUPTIVE FORCE 2 | HYPERCONNECTIVITY

Exploding technology has democratized communications. Organizations are struggling more than ever for control of their message. This power struggle for control of the story, and thus the brand, is one of the biggest challenges facing the practice of branding. Historically, those with the title of brand manager

> **MORE THAN EVER, THE SHAPING OF PERCEPTIONS IS BEING DIRECTED BY OUTSIDE FORCES.**

have been looked upon as the keepers of the brand. But, as the old Bob Dylan song laments, "The times they are a-changin." More than ever, the shaping of perceptions is being directed by outside forces. The notion that branding gurus, marketing departments, or any other entity within the organization can control its messaging is an illusion. As the world of communications becomes more and more democratized and skepticism increases, it's vital to understand that consumers are no longer passive receivers of messaging. The adage "the customer is always right" is achieving a new and powerful realization. It's the mantra for the consumer revolution. Consumers are finding ways to discredit or diminish the power and influence of brands if they don't meet the objectives of mainstream society. The truth of the matter is that organizations are at the whim of the public—and its scrutiny.

As trust decreases, reliance on opinions of people outside the company increases. More specifically, reliance on the *opinions* of peers. According to research from Edelman, a global communications marketing firm, a person is just as credible a source for information as academics or experts about a company or brand. This is proven by the fact that half of all adults are now routinely checking online reviews before making a purchasing decision (Pew Research, 2018).

The new reality is that experts who once pulled the strings behind the curtain must grapple with a brand-new world, where the veil once separating the organization from the public has been lifted. What is said, done, and experienced will be shared by a range of people inside and outside of the organization and across multiple communication channels. In his book *The Brand Flip*, branding expert Marty Neumeier (2015) sums it up this way:

> **"The explosion of connectivity and the power it gives customers is turning companies upside down. The question isn't whether your industry will be disrupted, but when."**

This is contrasted with the good old days of The Golden Age of Advertising, when perceptions were dependent on professional communicators who held a strong grip on both the message and the medium.

Bernays and the other Madison Avenue ad guys worked for companies with enough money to flood the communication channels with what they wanted people to believe.

The advertising professionals were experts at delivering emotionally charged messages that connected with the highest aspirations of people—and it worked. Slogans convinced people that smoking made you more manly or feminine, that buying the right appliances ensured you would be the perfect housewife, or that drinking Coke confirmed you were helping to create a friendlier world. These unmediated messages had tremendous power to shift attitudes and behaviors—and they did. The messaging hit the right nerve with people, but the

"THE EXPLOSION OF CONNECTIVITY AND THE POWER IT GIVES CUSTOMERS IS TURNING COMPANIES UPSIDE DOWN. THE QUESTION ISN'T WHETHER YOUR INDUSTRY WILL BE DISRUPTED, BUT WHEN."

advertising experts were also successful because limited access to communication channels kept those without the money or know-how from questioning or providing alternative "truths" to these carefully crafted advertising assertions. This is far from the situation facing communicators today.

Another challenge that branding professionals are facing—closely tied to the explosion of technology—is the information revolution. The sheer volume of messaging that bombards us today through multiple communication channels leaves many wondering if anything really is any different from anything else. Jay Walker-Smith, executive chairman of the research consultancy Kantar Futures, estimates that the Western consumer has "gone from being exposed to about 500 ads a day back in the 1970s to as many as 5,000 a day today." (Johnson, 2006).

Since kicking into gear in the 1960s, advertising has exploded into a mega-industry: "The U.S. was the largest ad market worldwide with an advertising spend of 197.5 billion U.S. dollars, followed by China and Japan." (Statista, 2018). The explosion of branded product and service offerings is overwhelming and confusing, leaving companies to face commoditization that's as challenging as what faced leaders in the 1950s. This glut of information is compounded by the number of communication channels vying for attention. Just as in the days that gave birth to the ideas of branding, once again organizations of all sizes are asking the question, how do we stand out in the crowd? The waning number of ways to create differentiation has caused an ever-increasing need to figure out new ways to create meaningful connections with their audiences, who are central to their success.

DISRUPTIVE FORCE 3 | SHIFTING EXPECTATIONS

It's clear that efforts that depended on power, control, and a disconnected populace are not the magic bullets they once were. If Bernays were writing the headline for the "brand-new world" we're living in, it would likely read, "Get Real." Even he would conclude that attempting to build connections *only* by pushing advertising messages or other forms of formal communications is doomed to fail. The opportunity is to turn attention to creating deeper, more meaningful, and more authentic connections with people—not just to convince, but to connect.

As the conversations about corporate responsibility and the importance of authenticity intensify, people are increasingly looking beyond the sizzle of product and service branding to the substance of the companies behind the image. "But this isn't about repackaging corporate social responsibility. Brands with a strong sense of purpose draw people in, aligning people inside the organization, while driving momentum outside of it." (Frampton, 2018).

What I observed at Interface was the power that shared purpose has to excite, engage, and motivate people.

> ## THE POWER THAT SHARED PURPOSE HAS TO EXCITE, ENGAGE, AND MOTIVATE PEOPLE.

The opportunity to do something they believed mattered ultimately created a culture that supported the development of innovative products and ideas that pushed both the company and their industry forward. This new energy also increased the attractiveness of the company to very talented people who clamored to work there. Beyond building deeper connections with its internal team, the vision that Interface shared with the world drew new levels of attention, trust, and advocacy from the marketplace. All of this in turn created a cadre of loyal customers and accolades from those inside and outside its industry. Is there a business case for engaging stakeholders with the core purpose of your company? Bet.

It's hard to pick up a magazine without seeing an article addressing the growing importance of values and corporate responsibility in attracting the best employees and building loyal customers—the lifeblood of all organizations. Savvy leaders get it. They understand that building purpose into their value proposition is one of the biggest business and branding opportunities emerging today. While many have jumped on this train, many more are waiting at the station, still struggling with *how* to do it. Caution is wise. While we see increasing validation of the need to embrace responsibility beyond philanthropy, failure to back up intentions with performance is deadly.

WHO ARE WE AND WHY SHOULD ANYONE CARE?

Final Thoughts

So just as Lewis Carroll wrote in Alice and Wonderland, it's important for organizations to understand where they are going—envisioning the future—before they can effectively create a plan to achieve it. Engaging people in organizations with the answers to the questions *Who are we* and *Why should anyone care?* requires value propositions that reach beyond the quality of products and services to the core purpose of the organization. But growing connectivity created by digital communications, combined with increasing skepticism, demands a level of transparency that proves authenticity of intentions through actions. This can only be achieved by creating cohesion between purpose and performance. Branding can play a powerful role in connecting organizations to the people they wish to attract. But new approaches are needed that reach past the traditional spin and sizzle that worked so well for Bernays and the other ad gurus who depended on externally focused propaganda-based advertising and public relations tactics to sway decisions. We are living in the Age of Conscious Consumerism, where it's not just about telling the story, it's equally about creating relationships and authenticity through actions that confirm the truth of the stories told.

The following chapter digs deeper into answers posed in the opening quote of this chapter, *Where do we go from here?* Answers emerge through shifting how we see branding and by adopting a set of management principles as the foundational beliefs of *The Next Evolution of Branding.*

"The answers you get depend upon the questions you ask."

— Thomas Kuhn

CHAPTER 2:
A NEW PARADIGM OF BRANDING

I am not proposing that everything we do in branding needs to be thrown out the window. The psychological tenets of **social identification*** that birthed the practice of branding remain a powerful force in influencing people to choose X over Y. However, what *is* needed is a paradigm shift that reframes branding through a new lens that more accurately reflects the shifting demands of the marketplace.

Through the lens of *The Next Evolution of Branding* organizations become brands that matter by engaging stakeholders in shaping, sharing, and living stories that reflect the highest intentions of the company and the people it serves. This involves fundamental shifts in our view of how we do branding (Figure 2.1). Those who embrace this new paradigm will not only

FROM		TO
WHAT WE DO	⟹	WHO WE ARE
SIZZLE	⟹	SUBSTANCE
CONVINCE	⟹	CONNECT
ME	⟹	WE

Figure 2.1. Shifts Required in the Next Evolution of Branding

*Social Identification is defined as a person's sense of who they are based on a sense of belonging to a group.

survive the challenges they are facing relating to the shifting view of the responsibility of business, the growing power of marketplace opinions, and the increasing skepticism of formal communications—they will thrive.

Shifting the focus from *What we do* to *Who we are* speaks to the importance of everyone in the organization feeling connected to a company's core purpose, values, and beliefs. From *sizzle* to *substance* reflects the importance of operating with integrity and authenticity by aligning behaviors with the values of the organization and the people it serves. Movement from *convincing* to *connecting* symbolizes belief in the importance of resisting spin in favor of engaging people in honest, meaningful communications. The final shift from *me* to *we* acknowledges that organizations are part of a bigger world, thus reinforcing the realization that every company has impact on customers, employees, and the world. Each person, each organization, has a choice to decide if that impact will be positive or negative. The movement from *me* to *we* also acknowledges that branding is not the domain of the C-suite or of any single department. Your brand is the co-creation of every person who interacts with the company—directly or indirectly.

Core Principles of The Next Evolution of Branding

Corporate brands that resonate with an increasing number of conscious consumers build cultures that live a brand that matters. *The Next Evolution of Branding* calls on organizations to respond to this opportunity by adding *responsibility* to the list of credibility, distinctiveness, and desirability, traditionally used to define strong brands.

Let's pause here to take a deeper look into the fundamental principles that underpin this shifting paradigm. Embracing these principles promises to build cultures that thrive because employees feel engaged and empowered *and* in turn this creates brands that are trusted because they are authentic. The first two principles acknowledge the growing importance of building *responsibility* into brands. The second two principles address the need to manage the hyperconnectivity and skepticism of the marketplace by recognizing the walls that once existed between external and internal audiences have crumbled.

PRINCIPLE 1. SOCIAL CONTRACT

Organizations have a *social contract* with society.

PRINCIPLE 2. MORAL COMPASS

A leader's most important role is to define the *moral compass* of his or her organization.

PRINCIPLE 3. THE BRAND ECOSYSTEM

Trusted reputations are created by viewing organizations as interconnected *ecosystems*. This whole system perspective replaces the outdated references to *us* vs. *them* by embracing the reality that branding is a process of connecting the "*we*." Everything is connected. Everything communicates.

PRINCIPLE 4. MOMENTS OF TRUTH

Organizations create reputations as *brands that matter* by building trust. This is accomplished by engaging employees in aligning an organization's identity (who we believe we are) with the expectations created by formal communications and experiences delivered at every corner of the organization—what we define as *moments of truth*.

Principle 1. Social Contract

At the core of brands that matter is the belief in the importance of organizations forging a *social contract* with society. Some of you may remember the concept of social contract from studying names such as Thomas Hobbes, John Locke, and Jean-Jacques Rousseau in your high school government classes. This belief revolves around the idea that we all have ethical and political obligations to every other individual in our society. Thus, the idea reinforces the importance of balancing rights and responsibilities.

While the social contract concept dates back to early philosophers, it is increasingly relevant to today's leaders, who are being challenged to examine their organizations' responsibilities to their employees, the communities they serve, and the world in which they operate—including the natural world.

There is a growing call from both customers and employees who are looking for something more from organizations. Yes, they want good products and services, but there is growing evidence confirming that policies reflecting a commitment to responsible corporate behavior influence the decisions of emerging generations about what they buy and where they work. In the future, organizations will be judged not just for the quality and price of their products but for who they are. This goes back to ideas advanced in the 1980s by the pioneers of values-based businesses such as Ben & Jerry's, The Body Shop, and Tom's of Maine, which first inspired the research I did with Interface. All were founded with the belief that it was possible to follow the dictum of Benjamin Franklin and "do well by doing good." These pioneers of responsible business translated this idea, not as a shiny veneer, but as a commitment to purpose that lived at the core of the organization's existence. Values and purpose defined their businesses.

It appears we have reached a tipping point in the collective consciousness about the responsibility of business. Old ideas that limit purpose to quarterly shareholder returns are being toppled. People are rewarding organizations that operate with a set of values that expand responsibility to triple bottom line measures, which includes their impact on people and the planet, not just profit. Even *Fortune* magazine, one of the most powerful voices in the business world, seems to be on board. The publication's "Change the World" list "is meant to shine a spotlight on companies that have made significant progress in addressing major social problems as a part of their core business strategy." (Murray, 2015). Alan Murray, *Fortune* editor, explains the magazine's reason for

> Do well by doing good.
>
> **Benjamin Franklin**

IN THE FUTURE, ORGANIZATIONS WILL BE JUDGED NOT JUST FOR THE QUALITY AND PRICE OF THEIR PRODUCTS **BUT FOR WHO THEY ARE.**

acknowledging these companies this way: "It is based on our belief that capitalism should be not just tolerated but celebrated for its power to do good."

Topics like corporate citizenship can feel abstract, but in reality, we are simply talking about organizations choosing to be a good citizen by operating with respect and for the mutual benefit of all. This means acknowledging the importance of the give-take relationship between a business and the people who keep the business in business—employees, customers, and the communities the business serves. The following excerpt from an article that appeared in *The Economist* offers insight into this connection (Davis, 2005):

> *More than two centuries ago, Rousseau's social contract helped to seed the idea among political leaders that they must serve the public good, lest their own legitimacy be threatened. The CEOs of today's big corporations should take the opportunity to restate and reinforce their own social contracts in order to help secure, for the long term, the invested billions of their shareholders.*

The author calls leaders to answer a question which on the surface is quite straightforward: How do we balance what's good for our organization with what's right for the larger society? The answer is equally simple: Leaders must accept the challenge to strengthen the *and* between profitability and purpose. Reframing purpose, not as a line in their mission statement or public relations add-on, but as a key driver of profitable companies.

The belief that a social contract should exist between business and society connects to what is often referred to as *corporate social responsibility* (CSR). This philosophy has its roots in business ethics and reaches beyond the idea that the responsibility of business begins and ends with philanthropy. In their book *Beyond Good Company: Next Generation Corporate Citizenship*, researchers Bradley Googins, Philip Mirvis, and Steven Rochlin define two criteria of the next generation of corporate citizens (Googins et al., 2007):

MINIMIZE HARM: This means taking account of and minimizing the negative impact of a firm's footprint in society. The main injunction is "do no harm."

MAXIMIZE BENEFIT: This means creating *shared value* in the form of economic wealth *and* social welfare, including reduction of poverty, improved health and well-being, development of people, and care of the natural environment. Here the message is "do good."

While minimizing harm is certainly a worthy starting point, the full potential of organizations as brands that matter lies in their willingness to move beyond simply doing no harm to doing good. What it means to be a "doing well by doing good" culture is unique to each organization. Not everyone can be environmental champions like Interface, but every leader and every organization can ask the question, How can we leave the world better than we found it?

Figure 2.2 offers a summary of the stages of corporate citizenship viewed through five stages. The progression shows the meaning of corporate responsibility evolving from the elementary stage where the focus in on legal compliance. These companies only give lip service to its importance. At the other end of the spectrum are the game changers, companies that have fully integrated the triple bottom line measures of success into their culture and are now using their voice as a platform for creating societal change. The Stages of Corporate Citizenship is useful in guiding discussions about where an organization feels it is and where it wants to go.

	Stage 1 Elementary	Stage 2 Engaged	Stage 3 Innovative	Stage 4 Integrated	Stage 5 Transforming
Citizenship Concept	Jobs, Profits, and Taxes	Philanthropy, Environmental Protection	Stakeholder Management	Sustainability or Triple Bottom Line	Change the Game
Strategic Intent	Legal Compliance	License to Operate	Business Case	Value Proposition	Market Creation or Social Change
Structure	Marginal Staff Drive	Functional Ownership	Cross-Functional Coordination	Organizational Alignment	Mainstream: Business Drive
Issues Management	Defensive	Reactive, Policies	Responsive, Programs	Pro-active, Systems	Defining
Stakeholder Relationships	Unilateral	Interactive	Mutual Influence	Partnership	Multi-Organization Alliances
Transparency	Flank Protection	Public Relations	Public Reporting	Assurance	Full Disclosure

Figure 2.2. Stages of Corporate Citizenship (Googins, Mirvis, and Rochlin 2007)

Principle 2. Moral Compass

One of the most important roles of a leader is identifying and modeling the values that define the *moral compass* of his or her organization. Like a compass we use to define stable and absolute

MINIMIZE HARM
MAXIMIZE BENEFIT

directions when embarking on a journey, organizations depend on their *moral* compass to guide decisions and to confirm they are headed in the right direction to reach their destination. The moral compass directs the decisions and behaviors of organization members by providing ethical guidance about what is right and what is wrong.

Prospering in a competitive environment requires attracting the best and the brightest employees. Embracing purpose and values that go beyond self-interest is of growing importance in building committed and high-performing teams. Establishing the moral compass starts with three questions:

QUESTIONS THAT WILL ESTABLISH MORAL COMPASS

Q1. Are we doing what's right for people?
Q2. Are we doing what's good for the environment?
Q3. Are we protecting the financial stability of our company?

Answers to these questions are associated with triple bottom line measurements of success. Brands that matter place these values at the core of who they are and are committed to constantly working to manage the delicate balance between them. There is no perfection. But keeping these questions at the forefront of every decision will keep everyone in your organization connected to its highest intentions.

By viewing your moral compass through the lens of the social contract (your organization's responsibility to its employees, customers, and the world) you can set the true north for your organization. Setting this direction is more than a "feel good" exercise. As part of the organization's creed, it becomes central to the value proposition of the organization.

These first two principles define important strategic discussions for organizations that want to connect with a growing group of customers and employees who are looking for more from organizations than just great products and services. The third and fourth principles explained below address the importance of aligning behaviors with the professed social contract and moral compass of the organization.

Principle 3. Organizations as Brand Ecosystems

Everything is connected and everything communicates. This view replaces branding strategies that are over-dependent on image development aimed at *convincing* with efforts that reflect an equal focus on *connecting* customers and employees with the highest intentions of the organization at every touch point of the brand experience. Building organizations as brands that matter is as simple and as complex as connecting the dots of what is said and what is delivered. This begins by acknowledging that brands are the results of an interconnected matrix of communications where customers and employees are equal partners with the organization in co-creating the meaning of the brand. This requires different attitudes about what it means to manage a brand.

Brands that matter remove false barriers between internal and external communications. They see the process of building authentic brands as choreographing the multiple ways the organization interacts with people within its walls and with its larger environment. They understand the strength of the brand is determined by the cohesiveness of the whole system. This is defined as the identity, image, culture, vision, and reputation of the organization. Through this lens the ultimate goal of branding is to create trust by aligning expectations and experiences. Over time this creates a corporate reputation that reflects the vision of the company.

IDENTITY. The organization's internal narrative reflecting beliefs about "who we are."

IMAGE. A collection of verbal, visual, and behavioral cues that influence the impressions and expectations people have of a company.

CULTURE. The assumptions, values, and beliefs shared by organization members. This collective understanding directs the behaviors of people in the organization. Culture impacts the experiences people have with the organization.

VISION. An organization's aspirations for the future.

REPUTATION. Effective brand management that consistently aligns expectation with experiences (moments of truth) creates strong brand reputations. Poor brand management that doesn't deliver experiences that meet expectations creates weak brands.

Principle 4. Moments of Truth

Powerful stories that tap into people's feelings remain at the core of great branding. But stories alone, regardless of how compelling they are, aren't enough. We live in a time when experiences are becoming an increasingly important part of the mix needed to build authentic brands. Creating a story that reflects the truth behind your name is crucial. According to Josh Feldmeth (2016), former CEO of Interbrand North America and current Senior Partner at Prophet, "Organizations that offer a powerful story, brought to life through the behavior of their people and products, will generate a higher level of loyalty and emotional engagement from customers actively looking for confidence amid uncertainty."

Establishing new approaches to branding that create emotional connections by shifting focus from convincing to connecting is vitally important. This requires building a culture where people inside the organization are fully engaged in delivering what has been promised in the messages designed to build image. These experiences are also increasingly important in the cluttered communications landscape because they are likely to become the only thing that offers the sustained differentiation needed to build an organization's reputation.

The simplest example of the importance of this connection is that of a restaurant advertisement that shows a picture of mouthwatering food, artistically arranged on a plate and served by smiling servers, only to have the real experience be a stark contrast: bad food served by unkempt and rude servers. Fancy advertising is a waste of money if the promise offered by the images isn't delivered. The sizzle of communications must be validated by the substance of actions. A good deal of money and time is spent by organizations that ultimately fail to build the brands they want to build because they leave out one of the most important success factors: engaging people *inside* the organization to deliver the expectations promised.

THE SIZZLE OF COMMUNICATIONS

MUST BE VALIDATED BY THE SUBSTANCE OF ACTIONS.

Final Thoughts

Thomas Kuhn (1922–1996), quoted in the opening of this chapter, introduced the term paradigm shift in his book, *The Structure of Scientific Revolutions* (Kuhn, 1962) to explain the importance of understanding the frames people use to solve problems. *The Next Evolution of Branding* outlines a new paradigm that helps organizations overcome the growing challenges faced in building bonds of trust by reframing branding through a new lens that gives equal attention to messages and experiences that define the brand.

The Next Evolution of Branding is built on a belief in the importance of engaging all stakeholders—the whole system— in shaping, sharing, and living a story that emanates from the core of who the organization is, what makes it different, and the impact it wants to make on the world.

The social contract and the moral compass frame the organization's commitment to purpose, which ultimately connects the values of the organization with what matters to customers, employees, and the world. Focusing on engaging people in the organization in aligning the actions of the organization with these deep-felt values is what produces authenticity. This defines what is needed to overcome the challenges faced in building both brands and reputations in an increasingly

> **PEOPLE WANT TO CONNECT WITH ORGANIZATIONS THAT STAND FOR SOMETHING AND THAT STAND BEHIND THEIR PROMISES.**

hyperconnected, skeptical world—a world where people want to connect with organizations that stand for something and that stand behind their promises.

In the following chapter, we'll look at this basic human need for connection as the invisible force that gives branding such power.

"We do not see things as they are. We see things as we are."

— Anaïs Nin

CHAPTER 3:
THE INVISIBLE FORCE OF BRANDING

Bernays was right about a lot of things, including the underlying psychological motivations that drive choices and the role these choices play in reinforcing how people see themselves. He was also right about how tapping into this psychology creates and strengthens connections between people and brands. This is the invisible force that has underpinned the success of branding for over 70 years.

The process of identification is how we as humans find our place in the world through the choices we make to be associated with certain groups, products, services, causes, or people and, equally important, through the things we reject. These choices reinforce our self-concept—our sense of who we are. As such, they stand as symbols, external validation of our individual identity. We wear a Patagonia jacket, purchase Interface carpet,

> **BECAUSE THE SYMBOLS WE HAVE CHOSEN EITHER CONSCIOUSLY OR SUBCONSCIOUSLY REFLECT WHAT WE VALUE.**

or wear the logo of our favorite sports teams because the symbols we have chosen either consciously or subconsciously reflect what we value. For some it may simply be the quality of the product; for others, however, the connection runs deeper, signifying our association with a set of values shared with other like-minded people. There is no greater loyalty than to those things that

"THE PROCESS OF IDENTIFICATION IS HOW WE AS HUMANS FIND OUR PLACE IN THE WORLD THROUGH THE CHOICES WE MAKE..."

START

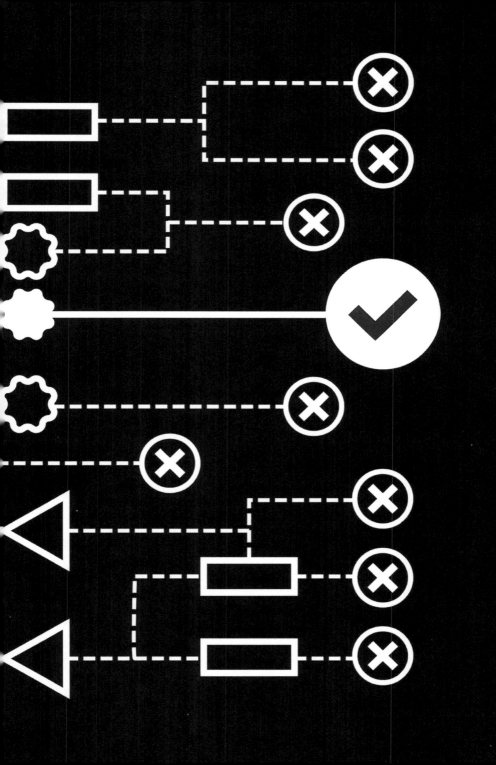

> **TODAY AN INCREASING NUMBER OF PEOPLE ARE MAKING CHOICES THAT REFLECT A DESIRE TO CONNECT WITH A SET OF VALUES.**

we have chosen as symbols of our personal identity.

In the 1950s, the advertising experts used their understanding of psychology of identification to excel at mining the desires of people to be associated with products that confirmed membership in a group that was sexier, richer, or even a little smarter than the next group. While these more superficial human motivations have not disappeared from the scene, today an increasing number of people are making choices that reflect a desire to connect with a set of values, perhaps a little more substantive and impactful, that are associated with the purpose of social and environmental responsibility.

In this chapter, we take a look at the concepts of identity, identification, tribes, and brand communities as the forces that forge connections between people and the brands they love to love. We will also explore the growing importance of a tribe known as Cultural Creatives and the parallel growth of a business philosophy known by many names, including Benefit Corporations, Conscious Capitalism, purpose-driven, and triple bottom line. Regardless of the label, organizations that follow this philosophy want to make connections with a growing group of people who define values alignment as a key factor in their decisions about who to work with, buy from, or invest in.

Individual Identity and Identification

Humans spend a lifetime seeking to answer the perennial question, Who am I? The answer depends, in part, on where and to whom we are born, but also on the ongoing process of testing different associations, ideas, beliefs, and values that we're exposed to throughout our lives. An important aspect of this search for self are the choices and connections we make throughout our life as we figure out what to incorporate into our self-image and, equally important, what to reject.

No person is an island, and neither is our identity. We define who we are in relationship to others. Seeking associations with people like us is hardwired, reaching back millions of years to when individuals formed tribes for survival. Traces of our need for tribal connection are manifested in modern society through our membership in churches, clubs, hobby groups, protest groups, political parties, social movements, etc. These affiliations serve as outward symbols that help people define themselves in their own eyes and in the eyes of others. Much like our forebears, our tribal membership is confirmed through the display of symbols and our participation in rituals and traditions.

While Seth Godin (2008) gets credit for popularizing the term *tribes* in his best-selling book *Tribes: We Need You to Lead Us,* as "a group of people connected to one another, to a leader, and to an idea in which they have faith," the concept is deeply rooted in the science of social psychology. Scholars Henri Tajfel and John Turner (1979) first provided important insights into the connection between personal identity formation and group identification through the concept of *social identity theory*. These scholars proposed the existence of a *psychological group*, which they defined as a collection of people who define themselves in terms of the same social category membership, what Godin refers to as the *tribe*. Identification enables these individuals to locate or define themselves in the social environment. **Other scholars**[*] have confirmed that people tend to put themselves and others into various social categories, such as organization membership, religious affiliation, gender, age, or age cohort as part of their basic human need for connectedness, empowerment, and immortality. Furthermore, "a member of a psychological group does not need to interact with or like other members or be liked and accepted by them. It is only her perception of being, say, a loyal patriot or sports fan that is the basis of incorporation of that status into his/her social identity."

Social Identity in Action

I love the TED Talks slogan: Ideas worth spreading. It's a great example of a brand that has tapped into the beliefs of a tribe. TED Talks were created to help people connect around the power of new ideas. When people join TED Talks or even watch segments, it's symbolic of their association with a tribe of people who are maybe a little smarter, a little more innovative and progressive. Selection as a TED speaker immediately elevates

[*]Katz and Kahn 1978; Denhardt 1987; Fox 1980

a person to being considered a thought leader—someone TED has vetted and deemed worthy of having an idea worth sharing.

TED Talks is an excellent example of a brand built around a tribe. You will notice that I didn't say a brand that created a tribe. Brands don't create tribes, but they can become symbols of what matters to tribal members—thus serving as connectors of people who share a set of values and beliefs. When the number of people who see themselves as members of a tribe increases, we see additional businesses vying to build brand communities within those tribes. Consider the fitness movement, which consists of people who are connected because of their commitment to maximizing their physical capabilities and appearance. They see themselves as athletes. This tribe consists of anyone from the elite athlete to the weekend warrior. Multiple brands compete to create loyalty with the largest possible number of members of this tribe based on the specific characteristics of the tribal subgroups: women, children, men, seniors, etc. Attracting a specific segment of a tribe to a brand community requires a balance between branding, which is all about creating emotional connections, and marketing, which seeks to balance the emotional side of branding with the more functional aspects of product attributes, price, and place (distribution of the product). We will explore more about how marketing and branding work together to influence consumer choices in chapter 8.

Tribes v. Brand Communities

Like many of the terms associated with branding, the words *tribe* and *brand community* are often confused. What's the difference? The short explanation is a tribe focuses on the values shared among members, while a brand community is built around a specific brand or product. The term *tribe*, as related to consumers, can be traced to French sociologist Michel Maffesoli (1996), who proposed that consumer tribes have emerged as a way to replace lost social structures. These tribes share moral values and opinions and are focused on the relationships among members. The Cultural Creatives referenced earlier is an example of a tribe in the context of Maffesoli's definition. On the other hand, membership in a brand community requires a more specific affiliation. Albert M. Muniz Jr. and Thomas C. O'Guinn (2001) introduced the idea of brand communities to describe "a specialized, non-geographically bound community, based on a structured set of social relationships among admirers of a brand. It is specialized because at its center is a branded good or service." More than just consumers, these people are advocates and promoters of the brand.

Let me share a personal story that illustrates the power of membership in a brand community. I'm a member of the *tribe* of people in this country who love football—in particular, Southeastern Conference (SEC) football. Even more specifically, I'm a member of a *brand community* loyal to Auburn University football. Here's my story:

I'm a big Auburn fan, and my husband is an LSU fan. Just in case there's any confusion, a sign hangs in our house that proudly proclaims, "a house divided"—with the Auburn logo on one side and the LSU logo on the other. For those of you who don't follow SEC football, this division is real. Mixing the two (at least on a fall Saturday afternoon in the South) is the equivalent of throwing gunpowder on a bonfire. One beautiful fall evening we attended the LSU-Auburn game at Tiger Stadium in Baton Rouge. As the game progressed, the growing score of LSU was only rivaled by the increasing anger I was feeling toward my husband, who was quietly sitting beside me. He was not obnoxious and didn't do anything that would elicit these feelings. But that day it didn't matter. He was the enemy. As the final ticks of the clock mercifully counted down, my anger rose. LSU humiliated Auburn 31–7. There was only one word to describe this Auburn fan's experience: painful. And only one description of my feelings: irrational. But as Bernays admonished, we humans are not rational beings.

This is a somewhat embarrassing but true story that serves as a metaphor for one of the strongest of all human needs—the need to differentiate ourselves through belonging. To define *us* versus *them*. Part of each person's life journey is the process of finding our place in the world. This involves connecting with some groups while rejecting others. I am sure, even if you're not a football fan, that you have some examples of connections you feel deeply because those associations say something about who you are. A deeper look at this phenomenon reveals some important and interesting insights about how and why people create allegiances. Insights that are important to understanding why some organizations are so successful in creating loyalty and advocacy while others fall short.

TRIBES

BRAND
COMMUNITIES

Brand Communities and Building Loyalty

So, what's going on? What compels people to drive around with little white Apple decals on their windows or Harley-Davidson logos tattooed on their arms? Or why do seemingly normal people wear shark-fin hats on their heads at Jimmy Buffett concerts and display bumper stickers proclaiming membership in the Parrothead community? Or, why do I still to this day get angry at my husband when LSU beats Auburn? And, equally important to our discussion, why do businesses such as Interface carpets, Patagonia clothing, or TOMS shoes have their pick of great employees, while others struggle to attract the best talent?

On the surface, my examples of Jimmy Buffett and Interface may seem very different; after all, what could a modular flooring manufacturer have in common with an entertainer? But beneath the surface they share a common thread. Their success has been propelled by the connections they've been able to forge because they offer something that people identify with and want to be a part of. Successfully creating these connections with people is not a function of size but of clearly understanding and communicating who you are, what you stand for, and why anyone should care. In other words, they have clearly defined what we in the branding world refer to as your core identity and value proposition.

We are Levi versus Wrangler; Porsche versus Tesla; Mac versus PC. As consumers, we make choices that align with our self-perception or with our aspirational self. According to Muniz and O'Guinn (2001), "brand communities exhibit three traditional markers of community: shared consciousness, rituals and traditions, and a sense of moral responsibility." Famous purpose-driven brands such as Ikea, Patagonia, Whole Foods, and the central example in this book, Interface, have created a brand community by building affinity with shared values.

Here's another personal example of how my identification with a brand has impacted my buying decisions. Given the market share of Apple, I'm sure that many of you will identify with this story:

> We opened the doors of idgroup in 1989. On the recommendation of our first creative director, Suzanne Raphael, one of our first purchases was a used Macintosh computer. Suzanne came to idgroup after serving in the United States Air Force, where she had been introduced to emerging graphic arts computer technology. She identified the use of this technology as a competitive advantage for us. She was right, but that purchase was about so much more.
>
> As I think back on the evolution of idgroup, I realize that the purchase of this first Mac was more than a simple purchase—at least subconsciously. We were the new kids on the block—determined not to look, act, or produce like anyone else. The now-famous 1984 Apple Super Bowl commercial that introduced the Macintosh resonated with everything we wanted to be. We saw ourselves as the little guy fighting the goliaths—just like Apple. We were the rebels who believed we represented a more innovative, bolder, and more creative product than anyone else—just like Apple. They were changing the world, and so were we—at least our world. The purchase of that first Mac symbolized our membership in this emerging brand community.
>
> Even today, when I see another person with a Mac, I feel a certain affinity with them. And while others have mimicked the

> *intuitive nature of the Mac design and have produced products that some argue are cheaper and do the same thing, I staunchly defend its uniqueness. Perhaps because it is so connected to our identity, we have never once wavered in our loyalty to the brand.*
>
> *The fact that Apple CEO Tim Cook is also an Auburn fan only reinforces my loyalty to the Apple brand.*

Tribes and Organization Identity

Multiple scholars have tackled the question of whether organizations have identities. They have determined that, yes, like individuals, organizations have collective identities that express who they are, what they do, and what makes them different. As individual identity helps to position someone relative to other people, organization identity helps to position the organization relative to other organizations. Communicating this positioning is the primary goal of branding; thus, understanding how organization identity is formed, maintained, and changed is critical to creating a culture where everyone in the organization is on the same page and moving toward the same vision of the future.

Researchers Albert and Whetten (1985) were among the first to define organization identity as a set of statements that organization members perceive to be *central, distinctive,* and *enduring* to their organization:

• Centrality: Identity as a statement of central characteristics that defines what is important and essential to the organization.

- Distinctiveness: Emphasizes that the identity statement should be able to distinguish the organization from others. This helps the organization to locate itself relative to others.
- Durability: Emphasizes the enduring nature of organization identity. This implies that identity is stable and difficult to change.

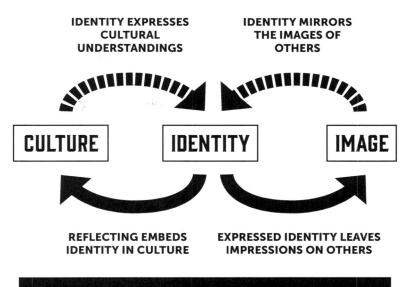

IDENTITY EXPRESSES CULTURAL UNDERSTANDINGS

IDENTITY MIRRORS THE IMAGES OF OTHERS

CULTURE　　**IDENTITY**　　**IMAGE**

REFLECTING EMBEDS IDENTITY IN CULTURE

EXPRESSED IDENTITY LEAVES IMPRESSIONS ON OTHERS

Figure 3.1. Identity Dynamics (Hatch and Schultz 2002)

Organization scholars Mary Jo Hatch and Majken Schultz (2002) offer a slightly different view of an organization's identity (Figure 3.1). They see it as being more dynamic and more open to change through interactions between the organization and its environment. The two researchers created the Identity Dynamics Model to demonstrate how communication loops impact how

BRANDS THAT
PEOPLE LOVE
HAVE CREATED
CONNECTIONS.
THEY'RE CLEAR
ABOUT WHO
THEY ARE AND
WHAT MAKES
THEM DIFFERENT

organizations define themselves and ultimately how those interactions shape the organization culture and image. These dynamics include stories told by the organization about who they are through formal communication processes, the experiences people have with the organization, and the impressions of others that are communicated back to the organization. The communication feedback loops from employees and customers support or reject the *authenticity* of formal communications (what is defined in Branding from the Core process as moments of truth). Over time, these processes of expression and feedback confirm the shared narrative and gradually embed the values, beliefs, and behaviors associated with that narrative into the organization's culture.

Identity dynamics was key in helping me to explain how Interface transformed its culture into Ray Anderson's vision for the company. There were many factors that created this transformation. One key was the authenticity of communications that helped build trust with people inside Interface and a growing group of customers (the tribe) who were looking for suppliers who demonstrated a commitment to environmental responsibility. What's important to note here is that culture change as well as changes in perceptions begin with shifting the identity narrative of the organization.

Brands that people love have created connections. They're clear about who they are and what makes them different—and they have engaged employees in consistently delivering on their promise. This reaches beyond just functional benefits—which are easy for the competition to duplicate—to the shared values that serve to create deeper bonds between the organization and its tribe. Remember, the tribe is not only the people who are your customers but also employees and anyone else who is essential to the success of your organization. In fact, employees are the engine that creates brand advocates. The more strongly the internal team connects with your organization's values, beliefs, and purpose—which lie at the core of its identity— the greater the chances are that your organization will be able to translate its purpose into performance, which in turn creates the trust that's a prerequisite for building confidence within the tribe. It's all interconnected, and anchored by people in an organization being able to answer the core identity questions: Who are we? What do we do? and Why should anyone care? This understanding, what we defined as *collective identity*, is key to building strong brands. So let's explore more about organization identity and how the concept is tied to tribes and the development of brand communities.

Think about your life and the products and services you buy or the social, political, or religious organizations you belong to. All in some way contribute to defining who you are or who you want to become. Savvy organizations understand this, and they use various communication approaches to tap into groups of people who are looking to connect with products and services, which those people see as symbols of what they believe.

Here's an example of how it works. Let's say there is a growing group of people, a tribe, who are committed to eating organic food. This tribe is preset to be influenced through advertising and other forms of communication that connect them with restaurants, farmers' markets, or other outlets that supply what they want. But if what's delivered falls short of their expectations, the trust of these tribal members is likely to be lost. Thus, authentic connections with people you consider your tribe begin inside your organization with your employees and operational decisions that reinforce the values that are espoused. By this we mean a shared understanding among all organization members about *who we are*. Embracing this collective identity allows creation of experiences consistent with the "talk." Failure to shape this understanding results in inconsistencies that in turn produce lack of trust.

> **EMBRACING THIS COLLECTIVE IDENTITY ALLOWS CREATION OF EXPERIENCES CONSISTENT WITH THE "TALK."**

Leaders often wonder why their organization lacks consistency, commitment, and employee engagement. In many cases the answer is quite simply that sufficient time has not been invested in connecting people inside the organization with the collective identity of the organization. This means giving employees something to believe in, connect to, and engage with. When employees experience this level of personal identification with the core intentions of the company, there's greater engagement, pride, and commitment that is revealed through interactions with each other and other stakeholders. Bottom line, the work becomes more than just a job. It becomes a personal expression of their identity, which is why branding should be seen as a process of creating connections with all stakeholders, not just customers.

Finding Your Tribe

For much of human existence, our understanding of where we belonged was limited by geographic location, but today our ability to find our tribe is easier than ever. The communications revolution that began with the mass production of books changed everything. While books have been around since Babylonian times, the advent of the printing press in the mid-1400s created a new way for ideas to be spread to the masses. This new connectivity exposed people to ideas beyond the physical boundaries of their geographic location. Today, new alliances are being forged and new tribes are being born. Affiliations are no longer dependent upon proximity or even on knowing other members of the tribe. We are in the midst of a new communication revolution, one that is in hyperdrive—technology has removed all boundaries, new connections are being created at mind-numbing speed. Our ability to find others who share our ideas, beliefs, values, interests, and passions is limitless. A Google search, a Facebook post, and a TED Talk are all ways in which we can align with others who share our deepest (or not so deepest) ideas and beliefs—without ever meeting them. While many of us in branding curse this hyperconnectivity and yearn for the days when we controlled it all, a slight shift in attitude reveals tremendous opportunity for those who understand the emerging tribes and what it takes to create brand communities inside those tribes. It's also challenging and frustrating for those who don't get it.

A Growing Tribe. A Growing Opportunity

Cultural Creatives was a term coined by sociologist Paul H. Ray and psychologist Sherry Ruth Anderson (2000) to describe a large segment of Western society that doesn't fit into the traditional categories used to define values, worldviews, and lifestyles in society. The traditional segmentation, based on attitudes and behavior, categorizes people into basically two camps: modernists/progressives versus traditionalists/conservatives. But Ray and Anderson's research (Ray, 2017) uncovered a new segment that they described as "bridge people," who are "trying to make a cultural synthesis, and also transcend the others." The two researchers assert that "values are the best single predictor of real behavior." According to Ray and Anderson, people who are cultural creatives have the following values:

» Authenticity: actions consistent with words and beliefs

» Engaged action and whole systems learning; seeing the world as interwoven and connected

» Idealism and activism

» Globalism and ecology

» The growing cultural significance of women

» Altruism

» Self-actualization

» Spirituality

Anderson and Ray predicted that:

> *Once they realize their numbers, their impact on American life promises to be enormous, shaping a new agenda for the twenty-first century. Their problem is that most of them never see the face of their subculture in the mainstream media, and that when they go to work, they have to check their values at the door. So, they rationally conclude, "It's just me and a few of my friends."*

Originally, the researchers estimated that this cluster of people numbered about 50 million adult Americans, slightly over one-quarter of the adult population, and an additional 80–90 million in Europe. Subsequent research (Ray, 2017) shows that the trend continues to grow (see Figure 3.2):

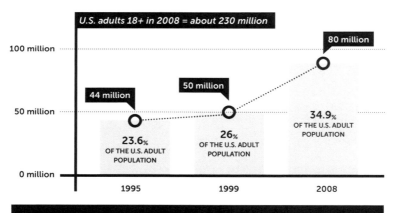

Figure 3.2. Cultural Creatives Growth in the United States (Ray 2017)

The predictions of the growing power of the cultural creatives is proving true—members of this tribe are quickly finding each other and collectively turning into an economic, social, and political force. This tribe has spawned the emergence of a new kind of business owner known as a *Conscious Capitalist*, who embraces a core philosophy of "doing well by doing good." Conscious capitalists are united by their belief that capitalism can be used to ignite positive change.

The ideas behind conscious capitalism can be traced back to Bangladeshi social entrepreneur, banker, and economist Muhammad Yunus, who was awarded the Nobel Peace Prize for bringing forth the pioneering ideas of microcredit and microfinance with his founding of Grameen Bank. These ideas were further elevated by John Naisbitt and Patricia Aburdene (1990) in *Megatrends 2000: Ten New Directions for the 1990's*. More recently in *Conscious Capitalism: Liberating the Heroic Spirit of Business*, written by Whole Foods founder John Mackey (2013) and his research partner, Raj Sisodia, who define *conscious capitalism* as "businesses that serve the interests of all major stakeholders—customers, employees, investors, communities, suppliers, and the environment."

As they continue to grow in number, conscious capitalists are unleashing capitalism as the catalyst for creating a better world by giving the values espoused by cultural creatives fertile ground in which to grow.

> UNLEASHING CAPITALISM AS THE CATALYST FOR CREATING A BETTER WORLD BY GIVING THE VALUES ESPOUSED BY CULTURAL CREATIVES FERTILE GROUND IN WHICH TO GROW.

Final Thoughts

The organization's identity is a powerful force that impacts how it is perceived. How the organization expresses its identity both internally and externally creates the affinity, defined as identification. This power of attraction the lies at the heart of successful branding. An organization cannot build an authentic brand without having a collective identity that's embraced by the members of the organization.

Cultural creatives are clearly a growing tribe whose members are looking for brands that reflect their values. For an organization to emerge as a brand that matters to these people, it must take the time to shape an identity narrative that reflects the core purpose and values of the organization. This can be done by answering the question, What impact do we want to have on our customers, employees, and the world? The answers are as different as the organizations asking the question. And the answers won't come from surface conversations but will require discussions that reach deep into the heart of your organization. You won't be able to fake it.

In the following chapter, we'll look at opportunities that organizations have for engaging with this growing segment of the marketplace known as Cultural Creatives and some examples of companies that are doing it well.

"The two most important days in your life are the day you are born and the day you find out why."

— Mark Twain

CHAPTER 4:
FROM SIZZLE TO SUBSTANCE

Over the years, branding experts have used their understanding of the psychology of social identification to excel at mining the desires of people to be associated with products that confirmed membership in a group that was sexier, richer, or even a little smarter than the next group. While these more superficial human motivations have not disappeared from the scene, today an increasing number of people are making choices that reflect a desire to connect with a set of values, perhaps a little more substantive and impactful.

Jez Frampton, former Global CEO of Interbrand, one of the world's most respected branding firms, offers this insight into the future of branding:

> If brands start and end with people, it's important to acknowledge a significant generational shift in the way people interact with, and what they demand from, brands. Both as employees and customers, younger generations have very different views about the brands they choose. They expect a brand's purpose and values to align with them, and their desires for better communities and a better world.
>
> **Jez Frampton**, formal *Global CEO of Interbrand*

Change creates opportunity. Companies can take advantage of the shifting market forces by becoming thought leaders and champions of the values that are of growing importance to the expanding tribe of cultural creatives. This involves tapping into the wisdom of Edward Bernays' premise that birthed The Golden Age of Advertising: by creating emotional associations between products and ideas, large numbers of people can be persuaded to change their behavior. By redirecting this underlying (and successful) psychology that was used to sell cigarettes in the 1960s, branding can instead be deployed as a force for good. In doing so branding can be a catalyst for creating positive change by creating stronger connections between people and companies that demonstrate a commitment to values associated with social and environmental responsibility. This opportunity reaches beyond just responding to an existing group of "believers" who represent a significant number of people, to becoming influential voices in shifting the mindsets and behaviors of others who are not yet on board. As far-fetched as this may seem at first glance, it's actually a logical proposition if we look at the potential of unleashing the psychology of branding to connect people with brands as symbols that represent their highest aspirations—for themselves and the world.

> **UNLEASHING THE PSYCHOLOGY OF BRANDING TO CONNECT PEOPLE WITH BRANDS AS SYMBOLS THAT REPRESENT THEIR HIGHEST ASPIRATIONS— FOR THEMSELVES AND THE WORLD.**

Growing Opportunities

As we discussed in the previous chapter, since the beginning of time (or thereabouts) what has remained a constant driver of the behaviors of the human race is our need for connections that reinforce our sense of self. Over the years, branding has proven a powerful force for creating these connections between companies and what people value. Increasingly, people are scrutinizing the values and behaviors of organizations as key determinants of employment choices and purchasing decisions. They are taking actions that confirm their commitment to values associated with the social and environmental health of their communities and the world.

A recent *Nielsen Global Survey of Corporate Social Responsibility* provided confirmation that the tribe of cultural creatives is continuing to grow. This worldwide survey of 30,000 consumers in 60 countries was conducted to better understand the impact of the values of corporate responsibility on the attitudes and actions of people. Here's what was found (Nielsen, 2014):

67% 67% of consumers prefer to work for socially responsible companies.

55% will pay extra for products and services from companies committed to positive social and environmental impact. **55%**

52% 52% check product packaging to ensure sustainable impact.

52% made at least one purchase in the past six months from one or more socially responsible companies. **52%**

 49% 49% volunteer and/or donate to organizations engaged in social and environmental programs.

BRANDING
HAS PROVEN
A POWERFUL
FORCE FOR
CREATING THESE
**CONNECTIONS
BETWEEN
COMPANIES
AND WHAT
PEOPLE VALUE.**

Strategies that connect with this tribe create wins in a couple of areas: first, people are looking to buy innovative products and services that embody these values. Meeting this demand supports the financial bottom line. A second win is created when organizations become places where members of this tribe can live out what they believe through their work. This results in organizations attracting (and retaining) their most valuable resource—committed, talented, and engaged employees.

> **PLACES WHERE MEMBERS OF THIS TRIBE CAN LIVE OUT WHAT THEY BELIEVE THROUGH THEIR WORK.**

The 2017 Deloitte Millennial Survey reported that Millennials (born between 1981 and 1996) feel accountable for many issues in both the workplace and the wider world. However, it is primarily via the workplace that they feel most able to make an impact by being a part of a collective influence through their employer. While smaller in numbers, Gen Xers (born between 1965 and 1980) also represent a significant group actively involved in volunteer activities; thus, they may be more drawn to organizations that provide outlets for involvement in causes they support. This means that there is growing evidence that building values of social and environmental responsibility into the core values of an organization offers a path to creating stronger connections with both employees and customers.

Those who choose to embrace the values of the cultural creatives will not only survive the challenges they are facing. They will thrive.

SPOTLIGHT #1

The Bottom Line on Values-Driven Companies
by James D. Ludema, Ph.D.
Professor of Global Leadership
Founder & Director, Center for Values-Driven Leadership

Values-driven companies do business the right way. Their leaders are clear and confident about their own values and they intentionally build organizational cultures based on values that promote flourishing at every level. This means everyone benefits: employees, customers, the communities in which they are situated, and the natural environment. These companies really raise the bar on how they contribute to the world by living their values.

We are talking about values like honesty and integrity, care and compassion, excellence and accountability, meaning, purpose, and contribution to the greater good. Research tells us that companies operating from a purpose-driven, values-based perspective outperform their peers over time in the marketplace. So, it's important to do, but it is also good business to do it. In the book *Firms of Endearment*, the authors show that companies with a strong sense of purpose and core values, a commitment to customers, team members, suppliers and community, real people-centered cultures outperform the S&P 500 in cumulative returns by 14x, and compared to good-to-great companies by 6x over a 15-year period.

Great Place to Work® produces the annual Fortune 100 Best Companies to Work For® list, and they show that companies high in trust, pride, camaraderie, and fulfillment among team members significantly outperform the market. The Ethisphere® Institute shows similar results in its annual World's Most Ethical Companies® list, which considers corporate citizenship, governance, innovation for public well-being, industry leadership, tone from the top, legal regulatory and reputation track record, and ethics and compliance programs. Collectively, the companies that score high on Ethisphere's list outperform the S&P 500 by an average of 7.3% annually.

CHARACTERISTICS OF VALUES-DRIVEN COMPANIES

» **They are clear about their purpose and values.**

» **Their CEOs serve as "Chief Culture Officers" to ensure a sustained commitment to purpose and values.**

» **They get the right people on the senior leadership team, people aligned with their purpose and values.**

» **They work relentlessly to integrate purpose and values into their organizational culture and stakeholder relationships.**

This is not a passing fad; it is an enduring truth. Great relationships are built on purpose, virtue, and values. They are built when people are honest and trustworthy; when they treat one another with dignity, respect, care, and compassion; when they invest in one another to promote growth, development, flourishing, and success. That's what makes for great relationships, great families, great organizations, and great societies. That's never going to change. What is going to change is how many people stand up and advocate for this better way of doing business. Globally, there are millions of companies, big and small, and billions of people who lead from a values-driven perspective. We need to tell their stories, support their efforts, and help make values-driven leadership the prevailing paradigm.

ABOUT

James D. Ludema, Ph.D.
Professor of Global Leadership
Founder & Director, Center for Values-Driven Leadership

James D. Ludema is the Co-founder and Director of the Center for Values-Driven Leadership and a Professor of Global Leadership at Benedictine University. He is Past Chair of the Academy of Management's Organization Development and Change Division and is the author of two books and dozens of articles on leadership, strategy, and organizational change. His book *The Appreciative Inquiry Summit: A Practitioner's Guide for Leading Large-Scale Change* is widely considered a classic in the field.

Daniel L. Goodwin College of Business
Benedictine University

Building Purpose into Organization Brands

At the core of an organization's brand lies a narrative that expresses how the organization sees itself and how it wants to be perceived by the world. Engagement among organization members with this identity is key in building authentic brands. As we discussed in Chapter 3, identity is formed by a dynamic process that's influenced by communications within the organization and between the organization and its external environment. Branding from the Core, discussed in detail in Part II, intervenes in the dynamics of this process by engaging stakeholders in co-constructing an identity narrative that ensures everyone is connected around a common purpose and identity. This narrative is used as a launching point for external communications that influence expectations and as a platform for shaping customer experience strategies; the relationship between expectations and experiences influences perception and, over time, the reputation of the organization.

The major story line in an organization's narrative is its brand promise—what we refer to as *the sweet spot of branding*. The promise lives at the intersection of how the organization defines the value it feels it can deliver and what stakeholders perceive as most important to them. The brand promise is a contract with the consumer that reflects what is important to both the organization and the people they define as their tribe.

Let's look at how one of the world's leading corporate brands is mining this sweet spot of branding. By incorporating its view of responsible business into its promise to the world, and then magnifying that promise through its brand story, Patagonia is creating deeper connections with the tribe of people they want to attract to their brand community. Patagonia's story checks all the boxes of a *brand that matters*. These brands are desirable because they are distinctive, credible, and responsible.

The mission statement of Patagonia captures its brand promise: "Build the best product, cause no unnecessary harm, use business to inspire and implement solutions to the environmental crisis." But Patagonia has also successfully tied this promise into a narrative about a bigger purpose that communicates the company's deeper intentions. This story lives front and center on the company's website (Patagonia, 2018a):

Our Reason for Being

Patagonia grew out of a small company that made tools for climbers. Alpinism remains at the heart of a worldwide business that still makes clothes for climbing—as well as for skiing, snowboarding, surfing, fly fishing, paddling and trail running. These are all silent sports. None require a motor; none deliver the cheers of a crowd. In each sport, reward comes in the form of hard-won grace and moments of connection between us and nature.

Our values reflect those of a business started by a band of climbers and surfers, and the minimalist style they promoted. The approach we take towards product design demonstrates a bias for simplicity and utility.

For us at Patagonia, a love of wild and beautiful places demands participation in the fight to save them, and to help reverse the steep decline in the overall environmental health of our planet. We donate our time, services, and at least 1% of our sales to hundreds of grassroots

> *environmental groups all over the world who work to help reverse the tide.*
>
> *We know that our business activity—from lighting stores to dyeing shirts—creates pollution as a by-product. So, we work steadily to reduce those harms. We use recycled polyester in many of our clothes and only organic, rather than pesticide-intensive, cotton. Staying true to our core values during thirty-plus years in business has helped us create a company we're proud to run and work for. And our focus on making the best products possible has brought us success in the marketplace.*

As demonstrated by Patagonia, purpose is a powerful story worth sharing for many reasons. Emotional connections created through storytelling engage, inspire, and empower people. Most importantly they engender trust when intentions are demonstrated through actions. From a pure business perspective, the perceptions associated with the strong Patagonia corporate brand mean that less time, money, and energy are needed to convince people to choose a new Patagonia product over what the competition is offering. The internal narrative of the customers goes something like this: "I trust what Patagonia stands for; therefore, I trust any product that has a Patagonia logo attached to it."

From a greater-good perspective, "Our Reason for Being" is a story that supports, validates, and inspires people to join Patagonia in making a difference. The story amplifies Patagonia's influence by inviting members of its brand community to join together for a collective purpose. Thus, turning something that can feel overwhelming when faced alone—fighting degradation of the natural environment—into a feeling among the brand community, that together they can make a difference.

A recent example of Patagonia's commitment to the values it espouses is a lawsuit the company filed aimed at stopping the United States government from reducing the size of the Bears Ears National Monument, established in 2016, as protected land. The lawsuit was filed in conjunction with rock climbing advocacy groups and other organizations. According to Associated Press reports (Gidman, 2017), the suit "says the proposed 85% reduction at Bears Ears is an 'extreme overreach in authority' and puts at risk dinosaur fossils and Native American artifacts, among other resources." Said Patagonia owner Yvon Chouinard to CNN of his litigious action, "I'm not going to sit back and let evil win."

While some may consider this risky business, it's quite the opposite. This example reinforces the earlier discussion about identification, tribes, and brand communities. Wendy Liebmann, CEO of the WSL Strategic Retail consulting firm, which studies the attitudes, mindsets, and behaviors of consumers, sees Patagonia's action this way (Price, 2017): "Shoppers see brands as their spokespeople. Many shoppers expect them to stand for something." In a world where we are inundated by choices, brands like Patagonia have been able to reduce the complexity of decision-making by delivering at the sweet spot of branding (Figure 4.1).

Here's how this translates. The name and logo of Patagonia have become a shared symbol for a brand community of people who love the outdoors and adventure and want to be perceived

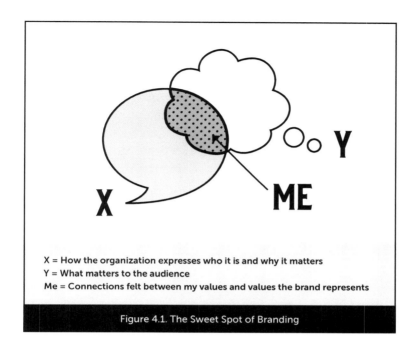

X = How the organization expresses who it is and why it matters
Y = What matters to the audience
Me = Connections felt between my values and values the brand represents

Figure 4.1. The Sweet Spot of Branding

as making a contribution to preserving nature through their purchases. Patagonia is an example of a brand that matters to this community because the company has been able to successfully align the organization's deeper purpose (of being advocates for the environment) with an adventurous outdoor clothing brand. People wear the brand to reinforce their connection to the values they share with Patagonia—even if they've never climbed a mountain.

The Patagonia example also offers an opportunity to return to the discussion about the connection between purpose, authenticity, and transparency. On its website, Patagonia explains its struggle to live up to its identity as an environmentally responsible company (Patagonia, 2018b):

> *We are in the earliest stages of learning how what we do for a living both threatens nature and fails to meet our deepest human needs. The impoverishment of our world and the devaluing of the priceless undermine our physical and economic well-being...In the end, Patagonia may never be completely responsible. We have a long way to go and we don't have a map—but we do have a way to read the terrain and to take the next step, and then the next.*

Patagonia is not respected by the world because it's perfect. The brand is recognized because it has boldly stated its intentions and is taking actions toward its goals while being honest about how far it has to go. Patagonia readily admits that balancing responsibility to the natural environment in a business that's based on consumerism is a tall order. This type of transparency defines authenticity and is what the marketplace is looking for from companies. Transparency has been one of the success factors in Interface's transformation as well. Intentions to become the vision that Ray Anderson had put forth for the company were shared through stories framed as a "climb up Mt. Sustainability."* Results of the company's efforts are published in annual sustainability reports and are updated regularly on the company website.

**Mt. Sustainability* was a metaphor Anderson used to define the size and scope of Interface's sustainability mission. It is still used today to define seven areas of improvement needed to get the company to its 2020 goal of becoming a sustainable enterprise. Interface has tracked and published its progress in these seven areas— the good, the bad, and the ugly—since the journey began.

SPOTLIGHT #2

Joining Corporate Branding and CSR
by Philip H. Mirvis, Ph.D.

Executives today are confronted with a dilemma: on the one hand, the public expects your business to behave responsibly, reduce its environmental footprint, and apply more of its resources and know-how to solving society's problems. On the other hand, it also mistrusts what business leaders say (e.g., spin) and the motives behind what they do (e.g., greenwashing).

So how do you respond to this dilemma? Consider the actions most firms take as they move through stages of corporate citizenship (or CSR). Typical first steps are to launch a few green initiatives, encourage employee volunteering, and demonstrate concern for society with cause-related marketing or a public relations campaign (CSR Stage 2-3 responses). Otherwise it's business as usual.

As a firm becomes more socially attuned (CSR Stage 3-4), it is time to upgrade the public affairs, communications, and CSR functions and to measure and report on social-and-environmental performance. Inside this integrates CSR into the business. Externally you demonstrate: "We take social responsibility seriously and hold ourselves accountable."

A select set of companies (CSR Stage 4-5) then take bolder action by incorporating CSR into their core purpose, products, and processes—and their brand promise. When do these efforts win cheers rather than jeers?

1. Be Authentic. The public is suspicious of companies that tout their good deeds—"Lipstick on a Pig." Unless it is authentically who you are. The top line of Johnson & Johnson's Credo states: "We believe our first responsibility is to the doctors, nurses and patients to mothers and fathers and all others who use our products and services." So J&J asked health care professionals about their most vexing problems and repeatedly heard "a shortage of nurses." It then launched its Campaign for Nursing's Future with ads featuring real nurses telling the world about their work and profession. It also engaged its staff and partners in fundraising galas and media events and launched nursing school recruiting efforts, leadership training for newly promoted nurse managers, and mentoring programs for new nurses. The results: The campaign led to a significant increase in the number of 18 to 24-year-olds who think of nursing as a good career choice. Recruitment and retention rates in the nursing profession substantially improved, too.

2. Get Employees in the Game. Nine in ten employees worldwide want to participate in CSR programs in their companies. Mentoring school children, cleaning up a park, or joining in a company "day of service" are meaningful first steps. Looking for more? Since 2008, IBM's Corporate Service Corps (CSC) has sent 3,000 employees in over 275 teams to nearly 40 countries for one-month service assignments where they work hand in hand with managers and staff in nonprofits, small businesses, or government agencies to solve serious social problems. Modeled on the U.S. Peace Corps, the program engages teams of volunteers in three months of pre-work, one month in country, and two months in post-service where they harvest insights for themselves and their business. What are IBM's motivations? To open new markets, develop a new generation of socially conscious leaders, and bring to life its corporate commitment to "Innovation that Matters—for Our Company and the World."

3. Take it Seriously. Does your company care more about profits than people or the planet? Danone, a world leader in dairy products, water, and baby nutrition, operates with a joint economic and social mission (a precursor to the "triple bottom line."). Danone's CEO has made a public commitment to reduce the company's carbon footprint by 30%. What commenced were a series of "lab to land" projects to reduce carbon emissions. In France, a lab was formed to reduce methane emissions by feeding cows with flaxseed. This had not only a beneficial environmental impact (reducing methane and thus the company's CO_2 emissions), it also improved the milk's nutritional quality. Hundreds of other Danone labs are featured at an annual review where country business units share innovative ideas from successful projects and lessons learned from those that missed the mark.

4. Bake it into the Business. A decade ago, Unilever managers scanned their world to assess the company's contributions to society. They identified hundreds of initiatives but no core thread among them. Months of dialogue, internally and with external stakeholders, led to the development of Unilever's "Sustainable Living Plan." On the food side, Unilever has dramatically reduced trans-fat, saturated fats, sugar, and salts in its recipes and been an early mover in developing functional foods—aka "nutraceuticals" with nutritional and medical benefits—with introduction of a low-cost iodized salt in India. As for personal care, Dove's "inner beauty" campaign promotes self-esteem for women of all shapes and sizes. Over three-quarters of Unilever's 170,000 employees say that their work enables them to contribute to sustainable living. And Unilever is rated #1 in its industry on the Dow Jones Sustainability Index.

ABOUT

Philip H. Mirvis, Ph.D.

Philip Mirvis is an organizational psychologist, consultant, and educator who serves as a senior research fellow for the Global Network on Corporate Citizenship. His studies and private practice concern large-scale organizational change, the character of the workforce and workplace, and business leadership in society. An advisor to businesses in the US, Europe, Asia, and Australia, he has authored twelve books on his studies including *The Cynical Americans* (social trends), *Building the Competitive Workforce* (human capital), *Joining Forces* (the human dynamics of mergers), and *To the Desert and Back* (a business transformation case). His most recent is *Beyond Good Company: Next Generation Corporate Citizenship*. Mirvis is a board member of PYXERA Global, a Washington, DC-based development NGO. Mirvis also served as former Trustee of the Foundation for Community Encouragement and Society for Organization Learning.

Mirvis has a B.A. from Yale University and a Ph.D. in Organizational Psychology from the University of Michigan. He has taught at Boston University, Jiao Tong University, Shanghai, China, and the London Business School and been visiting researcher at the University of Pretoria, South Africa, and International Executive Development Center, Bled, Slovenia.

Impact Beyond Size

It's not revenue, reach, or influence that place a company in the category of a *brand that matters* but rather the *why* of what it does. When most people envision purpose-driven organizations, they naturally gravitate to the big names like Ikea, Patagonia, or Interface, which topped the list of the world's most sustainable companies in *The GlobeScan-SustainAbility Survey* (2017). Or *Fortune* magazine's "100 Top Companies to Work for in 2018," which highlights organizations that have successfully built healthy, productive workplaces, such as the technology company Sales Force and retailer Wegmans Food Markets, which garnered the top two spots on the 2018 list. Or, they may think of a range of companies that use the principles that drive capitalism to solve social issues—known as social entrepreneurs. But how can smaller companies, those that don't have such a direct social mission embedded in their purpose, or that aren't as big as Patagonia, build responsibility into their culture and their brand? While all successful leaders understand terms like financial performance, operational excellence, and profitability, discussions about *responsibility* can be a bit daunting.

After all, what does it really mean to be a responsible company? Beyond this fuzziness around the meaning, this concept is often dismissed by smaller companies as being something that only large companies can really impact. But quite to the contrary, incorporating corporate responsibility into the core purpose is a strategic imperative for any business that wants to ride the shifting tide of attitudes about the responsibility of business. By making this discussion integral to your larger business strategy you can build a brand that matters—regardless of your size.

Furthermore, the influence of large players pales in comparison to the potential of the collective impact small businesses can have. According to the Small Business Administration (2017), companies that fall into this category account for 61.8 percent of the net new jobs created between first quarter 1993 and third quarter 2016, and they provide 47.8 percent of private-sector employment. Unleashing this segment of business to tap into the power of capitalism to create positive change can have a huge impact. I am one of these small business owners. Looking at how we and other small businesses have built responsibility into our brands may inspire you to do it too.

The *idgroup* Story

My team challenged ourselves to answer the question, How can our organization, a boutique brand-transformation firm, be more intentional about building responsibility into the culture and brand of our company? Perhaps sharing our story will help those of you who may be asking yourself the same question.

Everyone impacts the world, positively or negatively. Being aware of this and acknowledging that we all have a choice is the first step. Regardless of the size of your organization, you can use the following questions to begin a discussion within your organization:

1. How do we treat people?

2. What is the impact of our products, services, and operating practices?

3. What do we give back to our community and the world?

4. How can we use our voice and our story to be a positive influence on others?

5. How can we ensure the authenticity of our purpose?

Over the years, our answers emerged through steps that we've consciously taken. First, we examined our culture and work environment by asking the following questions: Are we treating our employees as we would want to be treated? Do our policies, procedures, and benefits reflect our belief in building and developing people? Are we helping people grow and supporting each person in creating a healthy, productive workstyle and lifestyle? Is this a place where people can bring their values to work?

A second area of impact is the choice of clients we want to work with. We believe our work matters, so we purposefully aim to connect with companies that we believe are making a contribution. By leveraging our impact through helping companies that represent our values, we can have a bigger impact. Thus, our values are central to our marketing efforts.

A more direct impact on our larger community emerged in the form of a program we developed several years ago called *Brand on Us*™. Annually, we open the opportunity for local not-for-profits to vie to receive a full Branding from the Core

ARE WE A BRAND THAT MATTERS?

1. HOW DO WE TREAT PEOPLE?

....

....

....

....

....

2. WHAT IS THE IMPACT OF OUR PRODUCTS, SERVICES, AND OPERATING PRACTICES?

....

....

....

....

....

3. WHAT DO WE GIVE BACK TO OUR COMMUNITY AND THE WORLD?

....

....

....

....

....

ARE WE A BRAND THAT MATTERS?

4. HOW CAN WE USE OUR VOICE AND OUR STORY TO BE A POSITIVE INFLUENCE ON OTHERS?

....

....

....

....

....

....

....

....

5. HOW CAN WE ENSURE THE AUTHENTICITY OF OUR PURPOSE?

....

....

....

....

....

....

....

....

rebrand at no charge. This nine-month commitment requires support from everyone on our team in addition to taking care of our paying clients. An additional complement to our commitment is the involvement our community partners—from media outlets to printers, programmers to caterers—who also donate their services. We lead the initiative, but it's indeed a gift from the community. In the end, we get to do some great work, and the not-for-profit has the tools to tell its story and make an even more significant impact on our community.

Finding the balance between doing and telling is critical to the process of positioning your organization. In other words, don't let your talk get in front of your walk. We've seen people err in one of two ways when building purpose into their brand communications, saying too much or saying too little. Along our journey we've occasionally erred on the side of saying too little. For a time, we were timid about incorporating our values into the information we shared with the world. Frankly, we didn't want to put people off by being perceived as "too granola." But that's changed. Today our values *are* our story. Yes, we do great work. Our team has many awards that attest to that. But beyond our work, we're committed to impacting the world through helping clients who share our commitment to being good citizens of the world. We're not shy in proclaiming our belief in the power of organizations as brands that matter to change the world. Don't be shy about sharing your purpose. Your story has the power to influence others.

THE NUMNUM STORY

Another smaller company focused on making an impact is NumNum, a start-up located in my hometown of Pensacola, Florida, and run by my friend Doug Gonterman and his wife, Jessica. During our discussion about their company, Doug explained that what they do is create and sell a pre-spoon for kids who are just starting to use utensils. The innovative design makes it less frustrating for beginners to feed themselves. But as we talked more, Doug explained that creating great products for young children is what the company does, but he sees a bigger purpose. The day-in and day-out hard work of running a start-up is driven by a passion he and his wife share to be a part of ending childhood hunger through their Bite for Bite initiative (2018):

> *At NumNum, we feel an obligation to join in the fight against hunger. That's why from the very beginning we developed our "Bite for Bite" initiative. As part of this initiative, we donate a percentage of the profit from every product sold to ending childhood hunger. While our product helps children feed themselves, it is also helping to feed those who need it most.*

Performance Excellence

Ultimately deciding what matters is a personal journey that must come from your organization's core values. But being a brand that matters involves more than connecting to a meaningful purpose. While Doug feels that his enterprise works for something more than just selling a product, his contribution to the bigger purpose of ending childhood hunger requires business excellence that drives financial success. I define this as *performance excellence*. Thus, the second piece of transforming organizations into brands that matter focuses on creating prosperous companies driven by passion and purpose but backed up by performance. This aligning of purpose and performance is the magic that draws people to brands. Think of purpose as the fuel that propels people and performance as the engine that moves the organization toward its destination. Purpose without performance will fall short of creating sustainable success.

> **THIS ALIGNING OF PURPOSE AND PERFORMANCE IS THE MAGIC THAT DRAWS PEOPLE TO BRANDS.**

If you're interested in benchmarking your progress, one of the several third-party certification agencies listed later in this chapter will provide a set of metrics that you can use to measure your impact against others. Or you can simply define areas you intend to impact, set reporting metrics to measure progress, and choose a method to report your results. You can also consider legally becoming a benefit corporation. Intention and transparency of actions are what is important here.

CREATING PROSPEROUS COMPANIES DRIVEN BY PASSION AND PURPOSE BUT BACKED UP BY PERFORMANCE.

The most recent action we have taken in our ongoing journey is an expanded commitment to the transparency of our actions by becoming a Certified Benefit Corporation (B Corp). This certification, which we'll describe in detail later, involved a rigorous process that benchmarked our actions against international standards. It validates our intent and provides a platform for the transparency that supports the authenticity of who we say we are.

WHAT IS A BENEFIT CORPORATION?

In 2010, Maryland was the first state to designate a new legal status known as the *benefit corporation*. As of this writing, thirty-three states and the District of Columbia now offer this as an option. These corporations differ from other legal entities because of their broader fiduciary responsibility. While traditional corporations are judged on the company's financial performance, a benefit corporation's performance is based on the company's social, environmental, and financial performance. There's no difference between benefit corporations and traditional corporations relating to tax laws.

Benefit corporations are required to publish annual benefit reports of their social and environmental performance. Each state's statute differs slightly, but according to Michael Vargas (2016), co-chair of the American Bar Association's Joint Subcommittee on Social Entrepreneurship and Social Benefit Entities, all of the state-reporting criteria include three core components: the corporate charter must contain a clearly articulated social purpose, the directors must balance or consider interests beyond shareholder profit, and the company must report regularly on its efforts to promote or maintain its chosen social purpose. Benefit corporations are often confused with Certified B Corporations (or B Corps), which are companies certified by B Lab, a nonprofit organization that has been certifying companies since 2007.

CERTIFIED B CORPS

According to B Lab (2018), "There are more than 2,500 Certified B Corporations across more than 130 industries and 50 countries, unified by one common goal: to redefine success in business." B Lab provides criteria against which the organization's performance, based on the social purpose identified in the corporate charter, can be reported.

> ONE COMMON GOAL: TO REDEFINE SUCCESS IN BUSINESS

For those of you familiar with green building standards, B Lab certification is similar to the LEED certification that's offered by the United States Green Building Council. The B Lab process evaluates a company's positive impact in areas of governance, workers, community, and the environment as well as the product or service offered. The certification results in a score. The value of the process is the baseline measurement it provides, which indicates where a company stands relative to standards set by B Lab for its industry group. The annual reporting requirement tracks improvement in each area. Each year, B Lab recognizes top performers through its Best for the World awards, which honor the top 10 percent of Certified B Corporations. "Companies that have scored in the top percentiles across a majority of the assessment's categories, based on company size, are honored as Best for the World Overall, and companies that have scored in the top percentiles in a given category, again based on company size, are honored as Best for the Environment, Best for Community, Best for Workers, and Best for Customers." (B Lab, 2017).

While it took some time to gather the documentation required, the assessment framework of B Corp certification helped our company, *idgroup*, to focus our attention in the areas of operation important to claiming this corporate status. The actual evaluation process gave us insight into what we were doing well and where we needed to improve (see Figure 4.2).

B-CORP CRITERIA DESCRIPTIONS

Environment

The Environment section of the Assessment evaluates a company's environmental performance through its facilities, materials, resource, and energy use—and emissions. This section also measures whether a company's products or services are designed to solve an environmental issue.

Workers

This section measures how the company treats its workers through compensation, benefits, training, and ownership opportunities provided to workers. It also focuses on the overall work environment within the company through management/worker communication, job flexibility and corporate culture, and worker health and safety practices.

Customers

The section focuses on whether a company sells products or services that promote public benefit, and if those products/services are targeted toward serving underserved populations.

Community

The Community section of the survey assesses a company's impact on its community. The Community section evaluates a company's supplier relations, diversity, and involvement in the local community. The section also measures the company's practices and policies around community service and charitable giving.

Governance

The Governance section of the Assessment evaluates a company's accountability and transparency. The section focuses on the company's mission, stakeholder engagement, and overall transparency of the company's practices and policies.

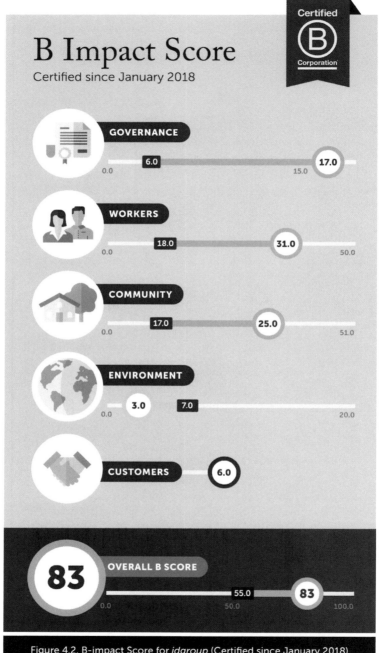

Figure 4.2. B-impact Score for *idgroup* (Certified since January 2018)

PERFORMANCE ASSESSMENT RESOURCES

For your reference, I'm providing a list of other organizations that offer third-party assessments and certifications. You should choose the assessment that's the best match for your organization's specific business goals. More information on these entities can be found at http://benefitcorp.net.

B Impact Assessment
The B Impact Assessment is a free, comprehensive, and transparent tool for assessing overall corporate social and environmental performance. Learn more about using the B Impact Assessment to generate benefit reports.

The Ceres Roadmap for Sustainability
The Ceres Roadmap is designed to provide a comprehensive platform for sustainable business strategy and for accelerating best practices and performance.

Global Reporting Initiative
The Global Reporting Initiative (GRI) is a network-based organization that produces a comprehensive sustainability reporting framework that is widely used around the world.

ISO 26000
ISO 26000 is an international standard that offers guidance on what social responsibility is and what organizations need to do to operate in a socially responsible way.

Finding the "Doing Well by Doing Good" Tribe

As the number of people categorized as cultural creatives has grown, so have the businesses vying for their attention. Unlike upstarts such as Ben & Jerry's, which was among the first to express values of social and environmental responsibility as core to its business philosophy, the new generation of businesses committed to doing well by doing good can easily find members of their tribe. The number of organizations and publications that are weaving a web of influence and support for those who identify with this commitment continues to grow. These organizations are creating connections and validating the decisions of those that have forged a social contract with society based on an allegiance to the social, environmental, and financial values that reflect the triple bottom line measures of success. They offer content-rich websites, workshops, and other methods to connect and support people who are on this journey. The growing number of members in these types of associations confirms that this approach to doing business is not, in the words of cultural creatives researchers Ray and Anderson, "just me and a few of my friends."

The number of resources available to connect, educate, and inspire is growing, but here are a couple of my favorites (the information is quoted directly from these organizations' websites):

1 CONSCIOUS CAPITALISM

We believe that free enterprise capitalism is the most powerful economic system for social cooperation and human progress ever conceived—when practiced consciously. Conscious Capitalism produces businesses that are good, ethical, noble and heroic. Our organization helps companies become more conscious with transformational experiences that inspire, educate and empower them to elevate humanity through business. By joining or supporting Conscious Capitalism, Inc., you can help create a world in which business is both practiced and perceived as the greatest force for good.

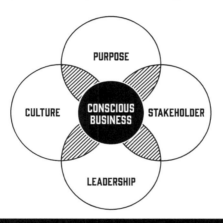

The Four Principles of Conscious Capitalism

2 SUSTAINABLE BRANDS

Replenish the World Through Better Brands. Launched in 2006, Sustainable Brands has become a global learning, collaboration, and commerce community of forward-thinking business and brand strategy, marketing, innovation, and sustainability professionals who are leading the way to a better future. We recognize that brands today have a unique role to play in both focusing corporate energy and also influencing culture. We seek to enable the success of better brands that are helping shift the world to a sustainable economy by helping them embed purpose-driven environmental and social innovation into the DNA of their business so that sustainability becomes a core driver of business and brand value.

3 | CONSCIOUS COMPANY MEDIA

Conscious Company Media shares inspiring, cutting-edge stories about business as a force for good, hosts educational events and workshops, and connects talented individuals with purpose-driven work, all with the higher purpose of elevating consciousness in the business world.

SPOTLIGHT #3

Insights from the Founder
Meghan French Dunbar

Conscious Company Media is the brainchild of two friends, Maren Keely and Meghan French Dunbar, who asked the question: Why doesn't a print magazine about sustainable business exist in the United States? The two had studied sustainable business in graduate school. Over the years they had witnessed the growth in the conscious business movement and felt there was a need to tell the stories of people and companies. In 2014 the two set off a new business venture designed to fill this void and Conscious Company Media was born.

I recently talked to Meghan about how Conscious Company Media reflects her personal "why":

My personal purpose is to be a force of love. Conscious Company Media reflects this purpose through helping to celebrate and elevate the entrepreneurs and business leaders who are working tirelessly to have a positive impact on the world. Not only do we celebrate these individuals, but we help business owners and leaders understand how to be more conscious leaders, create workplaces that work for all, and have a more positive impact on the world, which I believe has immense ripple effects for creating a better, more loving world. Most of us spend the majority of our waking hours at work. If our managers and team members are mindful of their behavior, if we have workplaces where people feel engaged and appreciated, and if we feel a higher sense of purpose through our work, we bring those values and feelings home with us and into our communities.

ABOUT

Meghan French Dunbar

Co-Founder Conscious Company Media

Meghan French Dunbar is Co-founder of Conscious Company Media. Prior to launching the company, she worked in nonprofit development and strategy for nearly a decade and received her MBA from Presidio Graduate School after studying Journalism and English in her undergraduate days at CU Boulder. Her passion revolves around inspiring and empowering people to create positive impact through their careers and businesses. Beyond her entrepreneurial endeavors, you can find her running around the mountains of Colorado, making the most of every moment, and trying to make people laugh along the way.

Final Thoughts

Sometimes phrases and terms such as *doing well by doing good*, *sustainability*, or *triple bottom line* can feel a bit esoteric, even confusing, leaving us wondering what it means to actually *do* business in this way. But on the most practical level, those who choose this method of measuring success have evolved beyond *being a good company* to *being a good citizen* by forging a social contract with society, which serves to inform the organization's moral compass. There are many definitions of what it means to be a good citizen. While doing research for this book, I found an exquisitely simple explanation titled "10 Ways to Be a Good Citizen" from the online classroom of Ms. Sanchez (2003), fourth-grade teacher. It's worth your time to ponder how you would apply the actions on this list to your organization:

1. **Volunteer to be active in your community.**
2. **Be honest and trustworthy.**
3. **Follow rules and laws.**
4. **Respect the rights of others.**
5. **Be informed about the world around you.**
6. **Respect the property of others.**
7. **Be compassionate.**
8. **Take responsibility for your actions.**
9. **Be a good neighbor.**
10. **Protect the environment.**

Beyond advice from Ms. Sanchez, stories from companies like NumNum, *idgroup,* Patagonia, and Interface have emerged as evidence that creating organizations with this approach to business is both possible and profitable. When Interface began its sustainability journey, it had no road map. The situation is much different today. Behaviors are now chronicled that show how organizations are moving the ideas of sustainability from philosophy to execution. Becoming a benefit corporation establishes a public statement of intent and provides a framework of expectation. Assessments and certifications offered by several organizations listed in this chapter set performance standards that validate those intentions. Research continues to

> **REPLENISH THE WORLD THROUGH BETTER BRANDS.**

provide insight into the characteristics that reinforce perceptions of authenticity, and finding the tribe of like-minded people to support your journey has become easier because of the organizations founded for the purpose of weaving this web.

In Chapter 5, we'll look at why culture is such a defining factor in corporate branding.

"Culture eats
strategy for
breakfast."

— Peter Drucker

CHAPTER 5:
THE OPERATING SYSTEM OF BRANDS

As I shared in the opening section of this book, *The Next Evolution of Branding* was inspired by the idea that *great corporate brands are anchored in the connections people feel to a vision that is meaningful to them. Their engagement with collective purpose creates a level of performance that cannot be forged by surface-level attempts to motivate people.* This translates to the importance of understanding that great corporate brands begin with creating engaged corporate cultures. While identity answers the question, who are we, culture responds to the call to PROVE IT!

Organization culture is akin to the operating system of a computer. Just as operating systems limit what computers can do, it's almost impossible for people to perform beyond the limitations imposed by an organization's culture. Understanding how culture works gives us insight into why it's such a powerful determinant in shaping both your organization's behavior and the perceptions people associate with your name. Understanding the interactions between the components of culture is key to successfully implementing the Branding from the Core methodology presented in the following chapters.

Management scholar and culture expert Edgar Schein helps us to wrap our heads around this rather abstract idea of organization culture. He does this by visualizing culture components, progressing from the deepest tacit or unspoken

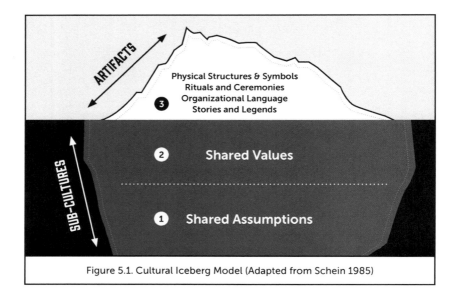

Figure 5.1. Cultural Iceberg Model (Adapted from Schein 1985)

understandings that people hold (assumptions and values) to the surface-level symbols that are the expressions of the culture that make these tacit understandings more visible (cultural artifacts).

Assumptions and values are deeply rooted in the history and traditions of the organization. While assumptions guide behaviors, values provide the justifications for actions. Together, these components of culture define a way of seeing, believing, and doing that over the years has proven successful and thus are worth defending and protecting. These assumptions run deep and aren't easily changed—even when the world around the organization is changing.

Understanding the power of assumptions and values on behavior is particularly germane to our discussion about the shifting responsibility of business. It's difficult, if not impossible, for organizations to change behaviors if assumptions about the purpose of business begin and end with the creation of shareholder value defined as profit at all costs.

Cultural artifacts are defined as the expressions of the organization. Schein positions these at the surface level of his model. Akin to the cultural artifacts discovered by archeologists when they study civilizations around the world, organization artifacts are visible symbols that give outsiders a peek into the lives of people who produced them. These expressions include physical manifestations such as buildings, office design/décor, and uniforms or dress of employees. For example, a pool table that sits in the center of an office inhabited by people wearing jeans offers some insights into the culture of that company. Cultural artifacts of the organization also include rituals and routines as well as other expressions such as logos, advertisements, press releases, speeches, and other forms of expression that reflect how the organization sees itself as well as attempts to influence the views of others.

Schein's description of culture envisions a daisy chain of interactions between the various layers of culture, each impacting and being impacted by the others. How these cultural components are wired together explains why people in organizations do the things they do (or don't do). The strength of these connections is what people mean when they say that an organization is hardwired to act in a certain way. This hardwiring can either advance or impede an organization's movement toward its goals.

An important prerequisite to any successful change initiative, big or small, is understanding how the current culture is wired. In a recent *Harvard Business Review* article, authors Boris Groysberg et al. (2018) identified eight types of company cultures.

ORGANIZATION ARTIFACTS ARE VISIBLE SYMBOLS THAT GIVE OUTSIDERS
A PEEK INTO THE LIVES OF PEOPLE WHO PRODUCED THEM.

The matrix (Figure 5.2 on the following page) categorizes culture based on the primary characteristics as follows:

» **AUTHORITY: BOLD, DECISIVE, DOMINANT**

» **SAFETY: REALISTIC, CAREFUL, PREPARED**

» **ORDER: RULE ABIDING, RESPECTFUL, COOPERATIVE**

» **CARING: WARM, SINCERE, RELATIONAL**

» **PURPOSE: PURPOSE-DRIVEN, IDEALISTIC, EXPLORING**

» **LEARNING: OPEN, INVENTIVE, EXPLORING**

» **ENJOYMENT: PLAYFUL, INSTINCTIVE, FUN-LOVING**

» **RESULTS: ACHIEVEMENT-DRIVEN, GOAL-FOCUSED**

This categorization emerged from the authors' analysis of over 230 companies across a range of industries spanning the globe. Their insights were gleaned from interviews with company managers and over 25,000 employees surveyed.

The researchers segmented these culture types along two dimensions describing cultures favoring independence versus interdependence and reflecting its openness to change, ranging from those who value stability versus flexibility (see Figure 5.2).

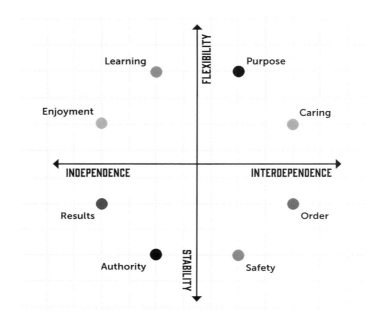

FROM "THE LEADER'S GUIDE TO CORPORATE CULTURE," BY BORIS GROYSBERG, JEREMIAH LEE, JESSE PRICE, AND J. YO-JUD CHENG. JANUARY-FEBRUARY 2018 ©HBR.ORG

Figure 5.2. The Eight Types of Company Culture
(Groysberg, Lee, Price, and Cheng 2018)

Within the four quadrants, the proximity of one culture type to others indicates characteristics that are more likely to comfortably co-exist. For example, authoritarian or results-driven cultures are less likely to easily embrace purpose-driven strategies; safety-focused cultures appreciate stability thus are more likely to gravitate to standardization and structure and may be less open to changes that require greater flexibility and innovation. Culture can be changed but it is important for anyone involved in a change effort to understand that the inertia of the status quo resists anything that falls outside of the box of the culture's comfort zone. I am sure you have heard it said, change is hard, and it is. But understanding the operating system of the culture will increase the odds of success.

How do cultures change?

Since we have established the importance of culture in building authentic brands, the natural question is how do you change a culture that doesn't support the desired vision and image of the organization?

When we say an organization needs to change its culture, we usually mean a shift is needed in the way things are done. In some cases that means surface-level changes are needed. This level of change is what organization scholars refer to as *first order change*. People in business define it as continuous improvement. This usually involves tweaking the systems and processes in order to do something better, faster or quicker; focusing on minor adjustments that make things better. An example from the medical world is reducing wait times by looking at ways to improve the way patients flow through the office. By first mapping the process and identifying log-jams that are causing the back-up, changes can be made to improve process and systems and, when needed, the roles of people in the organization. But first order change does not involve changes to the organization's identity or to the values and assumptions that live at the core of the culture. Words like continuous, adaptive, and incremental are used to describe first order change.

UNDERSTANDING THE OPERATING SYSTEM OF THE CULTURE WILL **INCREASE THE ODDS OF SUCCESS.**

This is contrasted with *transformational change*, which is described as "frame-bending" because it requires a fundamental reframing of how the organization sees things. This was the case when Ray Anderson introduced his new vision to Interface. Anderson's new vision "rocked the world" of Interface employees because it disturbed many of their assumptions about the purpose of the company. The process of resolving tension between the new expectations defined by Anderson's vision and the deeply held assumptions of the people inside the company is what we define as transformational culture change. One of the reasons the Interface research remains relevant today is that it gives us valuable insight into how organization cultures are transformed. At Interface, a new culture emerged by reshaping its identity narrative to gradually align with the new vision presented by Anderson. The process of creating behaviors consistent with this narrative, together with the acceptance of that narrative by the marketplace, embedded new values, beliefs, and assumptions into the core of the Interface culture.

This understanding led to the development of Branding from the Core as a whole system process of creating alignment between the vision, culture, and image of an organization through shaping, sharing, and living the organization's unique story from the storylines of its identity narrative.

The Link Between Culture and Storytelling

Since the days when cavemen strung together pictograms and tribes shared their stories around the campfire, humans in every corner of the world have used the art of storytelling to perpetuate their cultures. Stories serve much the same purpose in organizations. Organization stories, also referred to as narratives, are expressions that give us insight into who a company is, what it believes and what makes it different from others.

As demonstrated through the Patagonia example shared in the previous chapter, stories play a powerful role in building brands because they create emotional bonds with those considered to be the company's tribe. Sharing stories attracts customers to the organization but it also reinforces the understanding and connection of employees to the organization. At Interface, I observed how shifting the organization's narrative about who we are (identity) was the starting point for changing the *culture* (how we do things) and *image* (how others see us) of the company.

Aspirational stories shared inside the organization engage people in bringing a meaningful vision to life. Giving people room to figure out how to align new behaviors with these new stories is vital. Simply creating surface-level changes through telling a new story, without corresponding efforts to align words to actions, creates dissonance. In the South, we call this "putting lipstick on a pig." It may be prettier, at least in the short term, but it's still a pig. Veneers of change lacking substance are also referred to as *spin* or, as it relates to sustainability, *greenwashing*.

Regardless of the label you choose, it leads to dysfunctional organizations and perceptions of being fake. This is very detrimental to building the trust needed to be perceived as an authentic brand.

Transforming organizations into brands that matter involves tolerating failure and celebrating the incremental successes produced by the change process. We have also learned that when stakeholders are invited by leadership to be an active part of change they're more willing to commit their "full self" to figuring out how to align behaviors with the new vision of the organization. If over time new values and behaviors prove to be successful in achieving the goals of the organization, they will be institutionalized (hardwired) into the assumptions about "how we do things around here." In the Branding from the Core process we refer to this as engaging stakeholders in shaping, sharing, and living the brand story. As stated in an earlier chapter, people don't resist change, they resist being changed.

Leadership Values and Culture

The first two principles of *The Next Evolution of Branding* address the importance of the organization's social contract and moral compass. These reinforce the critical role that values play in shaping cultures consistent with the features of brands that matter (credible, responsible, distinctive, and desirable). One of the most important roles of leaders is as catalysts and champions for shaping and communicating these values.

Ray Anderson's awakening to the negative impact his company was having on the world expanded his view of the purpose and responsibility of Interface—expressed through a vision of the company as "the first name in industrial sustainability in words and deeds." This refined purpose helped the company to forge a new social contract and reset its moral compass.

Anderson was a masterful storyteller who became an evangelist for his vision both inside and outside of the organization. Internally, he was relentless in his determination to encourage his team to bring this purpose alive in the organization. One of the reasons he was successful in achieving this goal was his ability to weave emotional connections with the new values through stories and metaphors that everyone could identify with. Mission Zero that defined the summit of Mt. Sustainability evolved as a unifying language of the company; other phases like "play to win" or "the power of one" defined the teamwork and focus needed to reach the summit. An expression of the deeper motivation behind the Interface mission is captured in this poem, written by an Interface employee, that Ray read at the close of his speeches. *Tomorrow's Child* became the shorthand explanation for the purpose of Interface's journey.

Implementing Branding from the Core requires leadership to make a conscious decision to do what this phrase implies—intentionally shape an organization culture fueled by core purpose, values, and beliefs meaningful to those who are associated with the organization.

According to management thought leaders Tom Peters and Robert Waterman (1982), "The real role of leadership

TOMORROW'S CHILD

Without a name; an unseen face
and knowing not your time nor place,
Tomorrow's Child, though yet unborn
I met you first last Tuesday morn.
A wise friend introduced us two,
and through his shining point of view
I saw a day that you would see;
a day for you, but not for me.
Knowing you has changed my thinking
for I never had an inkling
That perhaps the things I do
might someday, somehow, threaten you.
Tomorrow's Child, my daughter/son
I'm afraid I've just begun
To think of you and of your good,
though always having known I should.
Begin I will to weigh the cost
of what I squander; what is lost
If ever I forget that you
will someday come to live here too.

is to manage the values of the organization." This requires a willingness to look inward. In other words, take time to allow discussion, reflection, and honest inquiry. Awakened leaders identify with the longing we all have to feel that we matter. They act on this understanding by using their organizations as a conduit for connecting both employees and customers to deeper motivations—beyond the *what* they do to connecting people to the *why* of their work.

> THE REAL ROLE OF LEADERSHIP IS TO MANAGE THE VALUES OF THE ORGANIZATION.

Organizations are *human* systems connected by much more than the lines and boxes of an organization chart. My experiences confirm the magic that happens when people are connected with an organization that inspires and excites them versus those that deplete their souls.

The opportunity is for organizations to engage people— from the hourly employee to the highest-paid executive—in feeling like they can be their best by bringing their best to a collective effort to achieve something meaningful. While money is one source of professional motivation, it's only part of the answer. Making a living by doing something we believe is the ultimate motivator. Creating a strong link between a purposeful vision and the collective focus and commitment of people is a powerful force.

As we will discuss in the following chapters, *The Next Evolution of Branding* calls on leaders to ponder the question: can organizations matter more by becoming places where people can live their values and where ideas are nurtured, grow, and thrive? Some would identify the ultimate business challenge presented by this question as staying true to the answer, while ensuring the generation of revenues needed for financial stability. I would propose that engaging people with purpose is the first step in guaranteeing financial prosperity. This challenges the view of profitability and responsibility as competing forces by positioning purpose as a key driver of performance and thus profitability. Branding's power to forge this connection is the provocative proposition offered by Branding from the Core.

Final Thoughts

This discussion about culture as the operating system of organization reinforces Drucker's perspective that culture eats strategy for breakfast. Strategy, regardless of how well-researched or well-implemented will fall short of results if the culture of the organization is not the top consideration.

This discussion of the connection between branding and culture brings us back to the guiding principles of *The Next Evolution of Branding*. Becoming a brand that matters requires engaging in dialogue about responsibility that reaches beyond just financial return to creating relationships that are mutually beneficial to the organization, society, and the natural environment. While there are many economic advantages and a growing business case for committing to the values of a brand that matters, be honest: more harm than good is done by leaders who try to fake it.

The next three chapters move beyond *should do* to *how to* transform organizations into brands that matter using the Branding from the Core methodology.

ENGAGING IN DIALOGUE
ABOUT RESPONSIBILITY
THAT REACHES BEYOND
JUST FINANCIAL
RETURN TO **CREATING
RELATIONSHIPS
THAT ARE MUTUALLY
BENEFICIAL TO THE
ORGANIZATION, SOCIETY,
AND THE NATURAL
ENVIRONMENT.**

PART 1 SUMMARY

THE MARKETPLACE IS SHIFTING. Gone are the days when organizations could hide behind official statements prepared by marketing and PR departments, or behind the glitz and glamour of ad campaigns. In today's world of conscious consumers, the need to address the increased connectivity and growing skepticism in the marketplace has resulted in leaders seeking a better, more transparent, more responsible way to do business. The solution relies on reframing the role of branding from a one-dimensional, departmental push initiative, to an elevated function that requires managing the whole organization's brand ecosystem.

In Part I of *Beyond Sizzle: The Next Evolution of Branding*, I shared with you the need for a new approach to branding, introduced you to the elements of the brand ecosystem, and described how igniting and embedding purpose into the mission and vision of your organization can have tremendous power in connecting your organization to a tribe of brand-loyal advocates. Armed with this level of understanding, shared in the following playbook, leaders will be able to begin the journey of transforming their organizations into brands that matter to customers, employees, and the world.

PART II BEGINS HERE

PART II

THE BRANDING FROM THE CORE®

PLAYBOOK

Mona Amodeo & Kristoffer Poore

THE BRANDING FROM THE CORE® PLAYBOOK

Transforming organizations into brands that matter to customers, employees, and the world.

The first half of this book outlined the philosophical underpinnings of why a new paradigm for branding is needed. In this part of the book, *idgroup* Creative Director Kristoffer Poore and I share with you an in-depth look into the framework and process coined Branding from the Core. Over the course of 15 years, this methodology has been fine-tuned to help leaders maximize stakeholder engagement, achieve clarity of purpose, and ensure that all members of their organization are sharing and living an authentic brand story. This process takes branding beyond the sizzle of the shallow, superficial efforts first introduced by the men of Madison Avenue in the 50s, to offer a new approach to branding that connects the sizzle to the substance that customers, employees, and the world are looking for today.

We refer to the following chapters as the Branding from the Core Playbook. In business, as in sports, a playbook refers to strategy for achieving an end goal. Teams use playbooks to ensure that everyone is on the same page and for team members to understand how they contribute to the successful execution of the strategy. Our goal with the Branding from the Core Playbook is to show how the principles of the Next Evolution of Branding can be moved from theory to action. As I shared earlier, I'm a football fan, and I often turn to the game and the people involved as metaphors for what it takes to create winning organizations. There are several characteristics of championship teams that epitomize what it takes to turn a group of people—all from different walks of life with different motivations and talents—into a cohesive team that crosses the goal line together.

Winning requires talented people, a good game plan that everyone buys into, an organizational structure that supports the plan, and adequate financial resources. Many groups have these characteristics, but nevertheless don't win. I believe that there are three key differences between winners and losers in football and in business. I learned these lessons from two of the best coaches I've ever known, Art Williams and Rickey Iden: Winners believe more, want it more, and execute better. These next chapters propose a game plan for creating organizations that display these characteristics.

The Birth of Branding from the Core

I came to the world of business after being a communications instructor and member of a documentary team at the University of West Florida. I loved the power of stories and wanted to help businesses tell theirs. From the beginning, *idgroup* was very good at delivering the sizzle. At the time, the name of our company was Image Development Marketing Group, which succinctly defines how we saw our purpose—we were an advertising agency. We did, and still do, great creative work. But like many others, we followed in the fooststeps of the Madison Avenue guys who were the evangelists of Bernays' views. At some point in the evolution of our company, I began to realize that the most important characters in the stories we were telling were being left on the sidelines. The employees responsible for delivering the sizzle we were selling had no input into the messages we were creating. Over the years, I had also listened to leaders bemoan their struggles to get their employees on the same page. The idea dawned on me that perhaps engaging people inside the organization in helping us shape the storylines of our advertising campaigns would not only create more authentic ads but could also build greater engagement among the people who would deliver on the images we created. But I had no idea how to make that happen.

The search for a better way steered me to doctoral studies in organization development and change (ODC), a field of management that focuses on human and technical aspects of creating high-performing organizations. More specifically, I was drawn to an area of study called Appreciative Inquiry (AI), which taps into the power of positive questions to engage people in uncovering the best of *what is* to fuel movement toward the greatest hopes and dreams for *what can be.*

The answers to questions that motivated my post-graduate work came together for me toward the end of my research at Interface. It was here that I began to see the connection between branding, change, and employee engagement. This insight offered answers to a more specific question I asked myself at the conclusion of my research: *How do we help organizations build the level of employee and marketplace engagement that I witnessed at Interface?* What emerged was a series of "aha"

THE EMPLOYEES RESPONSIBLE FOR DELIVERING THE SIZZLE WE WERE SELLING HAD NO INPUT INTO THE MESSAGES WE WERE CREATING.

moments that revealed a hybrid approach to building brands from the inside-out and the outside-in. *Branding from the Core* is a new methodology for creating an organization's most valuable asset—its reputation—by engaging its most valuable resource—its people.

Branding from the Core helps organizations win by involving the whole team in a process of shaping, sharing, and living stories that strengthen the relationship with current customers while attracting new ones. The doubled value of this methodology is the development of team members who are excited and engaged in their work because they feel that they can be their best by contributing to an organization that's known as the best.

This leads us back to where we started. As in football, creating winning organization brands begins with leaders who share a compelling vision, a clear plan, and a team that is a little more passionate, a little more committed, a little better at executing, and a lot better at adjusting the plan, as needed, in the heat of the game.

Just as in football, you can't win if your players are sitting on the sidelines. The following pages provide a playbook for building great brands by getting your employees fully engaged in the game.

**"Vision without execution
is hallucination."**

— Thomas Edison

CHAPTER 6:
BRANDING FROM THE CORE FOUNDATIONS

While many have talked in one way or another about the value of creating stronger links between people and an organization's purpose, the following chapters offer an actionable process for achieving this goal. These insights are based on the integrated perspectives gleaned over the past 15 years: 1) experiences with clients, 2) the synthesis of theories and best practices from the fields of branding and organization development and change, and 3) the Interface research project. Research and experiences come together as Branding from the Core—a *framework and process* for transforming organizations into brands that matter to customers, employees, and the world.

Throughout this book I have used the term *brands that matter* as shorthand to describe companies we love to love because they stand for something more than what they sell. They have earned a reputation not only for delivering quality products or services but also for being great places to work, for pushing their industries forward, and for striving to make a positive difference in the world. Branding from the Core is a catalyst for creating companies that live up to this definition by setting into motion actions that can contribute to small changes, or major transformations.

Each organization must define the specific details of what it means to them to be a brand that matters. Regardless of how the concept is shaped, the fact that three forces are disrupting the efforts of companies to build the "love" necessary to retain loyal customers and attract the best and brightest employees must be addressed. Each of the challenges, as outlined in earlier chapters, are framed below as goals of Branding from the Core. These goals are accomplished by bringing each of the principles of the Next Evolution of Branding to life:

GOALS OF BRANDING FROM THE CORE

1. Embrace the hyperconnected communications world through a whole system view of branding
   » Engage members in viewing the organization brand as a whole system—everything is connected and everything communicates

2. Embed an understanding of responsibility into the organization's culture
   » Commit to a social contract
   » Define the values of your moral compass

3. Reduce skepticism by building trust
   » Engage stakeholders in shaping, sharing, and living a brand that matters
   » Create connections between people, purpose, and performance
   » Build a culture that embraces the importance of creating moments of truth

Foundational Theories of Branding from the Core

While most branding approaches focus on telling stories to the external marketplace, they fail to tap into its significant power to create greater alignment between formal messaging and the people responsible for living those messages: employees. Branding from the Core offers a reimagined view of branding as a theoretical framework, an actionable process, and a foundation for strategic planning:

FRAMEWORK: THE BRAND ECOSYSTEM
PROCESS: THE BRAND TRANSFORMATION JOURNEY
STRATEGY: INTEGRATED MANAGEMENT OF THE BRAND ECOSYSTEM

Branding from the Core serves as a process for creating meaning that people associate with a company—the brand—through a combination of storytelling and employee engagement. The result is heightened levels of both the organization's performance and marketplace trust needed to build *brands that matter*. Brand strategy is viewed as an integrated management approach that ensures all the elements of the brand ecosystem remain cohesive.

THEORETICAL FOUNDATIONS OF THE BRAND ECOSYSTEM FRAMEWORK.

The Brand Ecosystem framework addresses the first goal of the Branding from the Core process, managing a hyperconnected communications world through a whole system view of branding. This framework is based on the ideas first introduced by biologist Karl Ludwig von Bertalanffy (1901–1972). He proposed the concept of open systems theory to explain his view of the integrated and interdependent nature of the various components of systems. The idea of open systems has been applied to multiple fields of study, but organization scholars Daniel Katz and Robert L. Kahn (1966) were the first to introduce it as a way to understand both change and stability within organizations. By taking von Bertalanffy's concept of open systems theory and applying it to organizations, Katz and Kahn introduced scholars to a new way of explaining how interactions, both within the organization and between the organization and its environment, impact the performance of organizations. Taking the concept of open systems theory further, in 2002, scholars Mary Jo Hatch and Majken Schultz introduced Identity Dynamics (Fig. 6.1), identifying the crucial role organization identity plays in organization performance. Identity Dynamics offers a way of conceptualizing how the interactions between identity (who we believe we are), the internal domain of culture (values and assumptions that affect behaviors) and the external domain of image (who others say we are), impact change and stability in organizations.

> A NEW WAY OF EXPLAINING HOW INTERACTIONS, BOTH WITHIN THE ORGANIZATION AND BETWEEN THE ORGANIZATION AND ITS ENVIRONMENT, IMPACT THE PERFORMANCE OF ORGANIZATIONS.

IDENTITY EXPRESSES CULTURAL UNDERSTANDINGS

IDENTITY MIRRORS THE IMAGES OF OTHERS

CULTURE   **IDENTITY**   **IMAGE**

REFLECTING EMBEDS IDENTITY IN CULTURE

EXPRESSED IDENTITY LEAVES IMPRESSIONS ON OTHERS

Figure 6.1. Identity Dynamics Model (Hatch and Schultz 2002)

Through the lens of Identity Dynamics, identity formation is seen as a result of interactions between the organization and its environment. Thus, organizations are open, adaptable, and able to respond to the environmental demands. This openness is what allows the organization to remain relevant to the marketplace. Such was the case at Interface. When customers asked "What are you doing for the environment," Ray Anderson responded with a new vision of Interface's future. This required the organization to evolve its image and culture to be more aligned with this vision. My research, built on the theory of Identity Dynamics, concluded that the shifting identity narrative of Interface (the way the organization talked about itself) was the catalyst that created changes in both the image and culture of the organization. This ongoing interaction between internal and external audiences ultimately redefined the meaning associated with the name *Interface*. As a result, a new brand in line with Anderson's vision as a sustainability pioneer was born.

Branding from the Core builds on what we learned at Interface by embracing the central role identity plays in creating the meaning people associate with an organization's name. In other words, a brand is created, changed, or stabilized by managing the various interactions between the organization's identity, image, and culture. In the Brand Transformation Journey, introduced below and detailed in Chapter 8, identity is articulated by engaging stakeholders in a five-stage transformation journey that shapes the brand identity platform and narrative used to create branding strategy.

THE PROCESS: APPRECIATIVE INQUIRY AND THE BRAND TRANSFORMATION JOURNEY.

The Brand Transformation Journey addresses the second two goals of Branding from the Core: the need to reduce skepticism by building trust and to embed an understanding of responsibility into the organization's culture. The journey is built around the phases of Appreciative Inquiry (AI) (see Figure 6.2). This positive change approach is used to uncover and translate the organization's identity into a narrative that is then used to build brand strategy.

Organization brands are unique and unfolding stories. As a proven stakeholder engagement approach for uncovering stories and engaging people in action, Appreciative Inquiry provides the perfect vehicle for shaping, sharing, and living stories that build authentic brands that people trust. Because stakeholders are engaged in this process, they are more likely to be invested in the success of the brand.

AI is a positive change management approach that evolved from an article written by Case Western Reserve University professors David Cooperrider and Suresh Srivastva (1987). The article argued that social improvement was being limited by current methods of "problem solving." Their solution was to flip the paradigm from the typical questions asked when faced with challenges: *what's wrong or why isn't this working*. This deficit-based thinking was replaced with questions that focus attention on uncovering what's working as a foundation for building new solutions. "More than a technique, Appreciative Inquiry is a way of organizational life—an intentional posture of continuous discovery, search, and inquiry into conceptions of life, joy, beauty, excellence, innovation, and freedom" (Ludema, Cooperrider, and Barrett, 2001). This view of human interactions has been used over the years, across multiple settings, to help organizations prosper.

The underlying premise of this view is that people move in the direction of the stories they tell. Because humans seek congruency between words and actions, the act of engaging organization members in connecting to a purposeful vision of the future ignites action. The focus is not on fixing what's wrong but on reaching new heights of success by building on what's right—capacities and strengths. Instead of the critical and negatively spiraling diagnoses commonly used in organizations facing change, this view frames change through the 5-D cycle

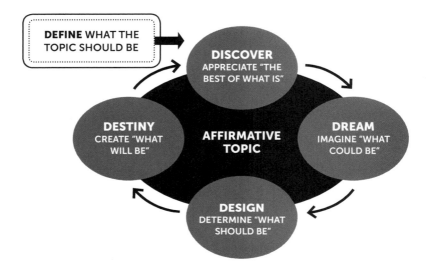

Figure 6.2. 5-D Appreciative Inquiry Model (Adapted from Cooperrider, Whitney, and David 1987)

of inquiry: Define, Discover, Dream, Design, and Destiny. Far from creating the anxiety and fear associated with some change processes, Appreciative Inquiry produces renewed energy, hope, and optimism by reframing challenges into opportunities to be seized.

The five phases of Appreciative Inquiry include(Figure 6.2):

» **DEFINE:** Stating the topic of inquiry in affirmative terms.

» **DISCOVER:** Uncovering the best of what is by focusing on peak moments of organizational excellence.

» **DREAM:** Imagining possibilities of what might be. The goal is to envision a future that's grounded in the core strengths identified during the discover phase.

» **DESIGN:** Shaping what's needed to build what was envisioned in the dream phase.

» **DESTINY:** Defining the actions that turn the vision into reality and sustain its vitality through the evolution of the organization.

The Appreciative Inquiry 5-D cycle is utilized in Branding from the Core to engage stakeholders both inside and outside the walls of the organization. The goal is to shape a shared narrative—translated into strategies—that creates the seamless integration of the elements of the brand ecosystem, introduced in the next chapter. This integration enables new levels of transparency needed to address people's increased connectivity, the skepticism of the marketplace, and the rising call for organizations to demonstrate greater levels of corporate responsibility.

In the following chapters, I'll dig deeper into Branding from the Core as a framework based on whole system theory and as a process that uses the principles of Appreciative Inquiry to ensure that the elements of the ecosystem work in harmony. By the end of this playbook, you will have the tools needed to embark upon a journey of transforming your organization into a brand that matters to customers, employees, and the world.

"When one tugs at a single thing in nature, he finds it is attached to the rest of the world. "

— John Muir

CHAPTER 7:
THE FRAMEWORK: THE BRAND ECOSYSTEM

The central idea behind *Beyond Sizzle: The Next Evolution of Branding* is captured in a quote from branding pioneer Wally Olins that was featured in the British newspaper *The Guardian* upon his death in 2014: "Branding is an altogether higher-order, more holistic concern, nothing less than an organising principle for practically everything a business or organisation did." This perspective reflects a view of organizations in which every touch point is important to creating brands—not only what's said but also what's experienced. I believe Wally got it right.

I tackled the challenge of translating Olins' view of branding (an approach to organizing) into something more actionable. I was inspired by the work of Janine Benyus, the co-founder of the Biomimicry Institute, who solves some of the biggest challenges facing business by asking, "What would nature do?" I found answers to my questions in the most perfect design example we have—the ecosystems found in the natural environment.

An ecosystem is a community of organisms and their environment functioning in harmony. The various parts of an ecosystem work seamlessly as a whole—each element impacts, and is impacted by, the others. For example, in order to thrive,

THE VARIOUS PARTS OF AN ECOSYSTEM WORK SEAMLESSLY AS A WHOLE.

a coral reef depends on the depth of the reef in the water, amount of sunlight, and water flow to move nutrients. These factors, together with the temperature of the water and the bio matter (fish and other organisms), support the recycling of nutrients such as nitrogen, oxygen, and salt. Combined, the integration of these factors determines the health of the system, and everything thrives when there's balance. But the entire system risks collapse if the balance is broken. As in nature, each component of the brand ecosystem plays a unique role in creating perceptions, but all must work together for the system to thrive.

By combining Olins's view of branding as an organizing principle and Benyus's inspiration from nature, we re-frame the concept of brand strategy as a plan for choreographing the interacting components of the organization that impact the brand—the *brand ecosystem*. Imagining organizations as brand ecosystems acknowledges the living nature of brands. Additionally, it reinforces the importance of engaging every corner of the organization in creating meaningful experiences that define the brand. This represents an important shift from viewing branding as a function owned by marketing departments or experts who are charged with pushing out messaging, to one that sees branding as dependent on engaging all stakeholders in shaping the meaning that defines the brand.

Olins' comments inspired a whole system view of brands, and Benyus the metaphor of organizations as brand ecosystems, but as I shared in the previous chapter, the Brand Ecosystem framework (see Figure 7.1) is built upon the theory of Identity Dynamics developed by researchers Hatch and Schultz (2002).

As such, the dynamics of identity (interactions between image and culture) is positioned in the brand ecosystem as the connector in building, stabilizing, or changing brands, and ultimately in influencing an organization's reputation.

Building on the ideas of open system theory introduced in Chapter 6, this branding framework replaces the traditional, segmented silos of internal versus external brand communication with a whole system—a highly connected matrix in which a brand is shaped through the dynamic interaction of its parts. Like any healthy ecosystem, each part has its unique role, but all must function as a whole in order for the system—or in this case, the brand—to thrive.

The illustration in Figure 7.1 defines the components of the brand ecosystem—identity, vision, culture, and image—within the context of the system's operating environment. It's important to see these elements as dynamic: each impacting and being impacted by the other. Everything is connected. Everything communicates. Healthy organizations, like healthy ecosystems in nature, function at their highest level when there's congruity between the elements of the system. As the collective response to the question, *who are we,* the identity component of the brand ecosystem framework reflects the organization's self-concept. Identity is positioned in the center of the ecosystem framework as a circle that connects all of the other parts; a powerful force in facilitating congruity between the image, culture, and vision of the organization.

THE BRAND ECOSYSTEM

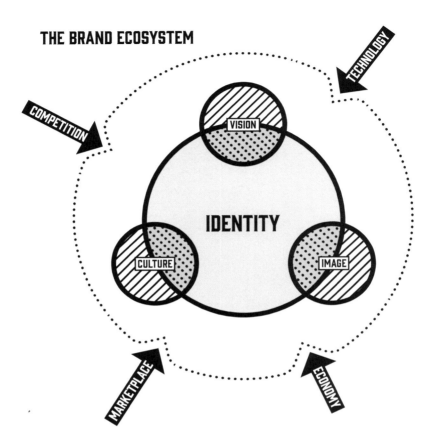

COMPETITION

TECHNOLOGY

VISION

IDENTITY

CULTURE

IMAGE

MARKETPLACE

ECONOMY

 EXPRESSION OF THE IDENTITY NARRATIVE (AFFECT)
Communications and actions that reflect the intentions of the organization—how it desires to be perceived—expressed through image development and customer experiences.

 IMPRESSION (EFFECT)
Perceptions held by customers, employees, and the world about the organization.

 OUTSIDE PRESSURES (ENVIRONMENT)
Context in which the organization operates.

Figure 7.1. The Brand Ecosystem Model (Adapted from Hatch and Schultz 2002)

The Brand Ecosystem, Defined

The following pages provide an explanation of the components of the brand ecosystem that must be choreographed to build brands that are both relevant and authentic.

OPERATING CONTEXT. Organizations are not islands. They must operate within a bigger environment in which they exist. This operating context appears in the brand ecosystem model as the externalities pushing upon the system. Understanding these factors is important in creating a brand strategy that supports organizations in remaining healthy and relevant. These forces include: the marketplace (*what are consumers looking for?*), the economy (*what are the financial constraints?*), the competition (*who are our key competitors?*), and finally the impact of technology on all of these interactions. Since branding is by definition a process of positioning your organization (as well as its products or services) as sufficiently different from and more valuable than what others offer, understanding where the organization fits within its operating environment is an essential first step in the branding process.

While understanding internal perspectives of members and having a clear vision for the future are essential building blocks of healthy brands, failure to consider the bigger context can be fatal. Thus, a central tenet of Branding from the Core is the importance of continuously monitoring the external environment to determine what is working and what needs to change in order for the organization to remain relevant. Your organization doesn't want be known for building horse-drawn carriages in a world that's looking for electric cars, regardless of how good you are at building those carriages. Too much of an inward focus can put even the most durable brands at risk because they fail to listen and respond to the external messages coming from those vital to their success. However, being overly reactive can cause confusion, leaving people asking, *just who are you?*

In the next chapter, I will introduce the SOAR analysis (Strengths, Opportunities, Aspirations, and Results) that is conducted in the first stage of the Brand Transformation Journey to help uncover the relationship of the organization within the context of its operating system. This external view, combined with the internal perspectives generated during the Branding from the Core process, will help leaders create strategies for building a brand that is authentic, relevant, and competitive.

1 VISION

Vision is the organization's North Star. It's a mental model that defines a future state that is both meaningful and worthwhile to the organization. An organization's vision translates the hopes and dreams of the organization in a way that engages the imagination and inspires action. An effective vision escapes the confines of the page to become embedded in the everyday conversations and behaviors of the people in the organization. Since vision statements are aspirational by design, they should be broad and far-reaching enough to set a goal worth achieving. A healthy dose of anxiety created by the gap between where you are and where you want to be is what motivates the organization's members to continually innovate. The more purposeful the vision, the more inspired people are, and the more engaged they will be in helping the organization realize its full potential.

2 | IDENTITY

Organization identity is defined as the collective understanding of people in the organization about "who we are." Identity within the brand ecosystem is captured through development of an identity narrative.

Organization identities evolve much the same way as our individual identities. Organization identity, like personal identity, is partly constructed by the organization's sense of "who we are," but also by the opinions of others. Organization identity is expressed through messages conveyed in images, words, and actions. If these expressions are viewed positively by the people who are important to the organization, this provides the reinforcement and acceptance needed for them to continue these new expressions.

On the individual level, our psychological health is dependent upon the degree of congruity between our self-perception, our actions, and others' perceptions of us. If at some point we experience a shift in what's important to us, or if we decide that we want a different group to accept us, then we set out to find new ways to express ourselves so that how we're perceived aligns with this aspirational self. The same is true for organizations. You may have observed this when individuals or organizations reinvent themselves because of a desire to be perceived differently. This is what we define as *rebranding*. You may have also experienced situations in which there's misalignment between what you see, what you hear, and what you experience. In both individuals and organizations, this creates stress and distrust.

The obvious difference between organization identity and personal identity is that organizations have the challenge of bringing together diverse people, each with an individual identity, to create a *collective identity*. A challenge that is addressed in the dialogue phase of the Brand Transformation Journey.

3 | IMAGE

An organization's image is reflected in the world's overall impression of the company. Through the lens of Branding from the Core, image is defined as how the world responds to the questions, "who are you?" and "why should I care?" While image can't be controlled, image development strategies can influence perceptions through planned communications that aim to create a tight coupling between what the organization wants people to believe and what people perceive. This encompasses various forms of communications, including the naming, logos, and other forms of visual branding, design of collateral materials, and the shaping of advertising, public relations, social media, and promotional messages.

4 | CULTURE

The collection of assumptions, values, and beliefs shared by the organization members that reflect an understanding of *"how we do things around here,"* defines culture. Culture is intangible yet omnipresent in all organizations. An organization's culture can propel or hinder the branding process because it exerts such a strong influence over the behaviors of employees and, thus, the experiences of the customers and employees.

We understand an organization's culture by observing the behaviors, attitudes, and actions of its members as well as the tangible artifacts its produces. As part of the Branding from the Core process, strategies are developed to influence culture through internal storytelling and performance standards that reinforce the organization's identity narrative. Over time, desired behaviors and beliefs, if reinforced by those important to the organization's success, become embedded in the hearts and minds of employees as "the way we do things," thus becoming part of what is referred to as *organization culture.*

AN ORGANIZATION'S CULTURE CAN PROPEL OR HINDER THE BRANDING PROCESS BECAUSE IT EXERTS SUCH A STRONG INFLUENCE OVER THE BEHAVIORS OF EMPLOYEES, AND THUS, THE EXPERIENCES OF THE CUSTOMERS AND EMPLOYEES.

---

5 REPUTATION

Reputation evolves over time as a collection of perceptions and judgments people have as a result of both the images portrayed by the organization and the experiences people have either directly or indirectly with it. This differs from an organization's image in that image is more fleeting and transitory and more open to change, while reputation is more collective, more stable, and ultimately more valuable to the organization.

Desired reputations are created through the effective management of the brand ecosystem, over time. The cohesiveness between an organization's identity narrative, image, culture, and vision ensures consistent alignment of expectations and experiences, and in turn the creation of trust and advocacy defined by Branding from the Core as *return on reputation*.

Return on Reputation

Field research has established the importance of aligning these dynamic components of the ecosystem in the development of brands. "Our research into 100 companies around the world over ten years shows that a company must align three essential, interdependent elements—call them strategic stars—to create a strong corporate brand: vision, culture, and image." (Hatch and Schultz, *Harvard Business Review* 2001).

Key findings from these researchers teach us about how the linkages between identity, image, and culture contribute to creating change (and stability) in organizations, as well as what is needed to build strong corporate or organization brands (Hatch and Schultz, 2000, 2001, 2002, 2008). The degree of alignment between these elements is an important factor in building the authenticity and trust needed to overcome the skepticism of the marketplace that we discussed in the opening chapters of this book.

From a brand management perspective, the goal is to maintain the alignment between leadership's vision of the future and *who we say we are* (identity), *what others believe we are* (image) and *what people experience when interacting with the organization* (culture), all while remaining open to changes in what is important to the marketplace. The more alignment between identity, image, culture, and the wants, needs, and desires of the marketplace, the more relevant the organization becomes. Over time this results in a trusted brand reputation. This is the ultimate goal of Branding from the Core.

But exactly *how* do we align the components of the ecosystem? In the following chapter, I'll explain the Brand Transformation Journey as the process for uncovering and articulating this collective identity. This is accomplished through the creation of the identity platform and narrative, as the expression of how the organization defines itself, as well as how it wants to be seen by others. The identity narrative, crafted by stakeholders, is the first step in creating strategies that influence the images held by external audiences while reinforcing or changing the cultural understanding of organization members. From this perspective, identity is the magnetic force that holds together the authenticity of brands. This is what I mean by the statement I made in the opening pages of this book: Branding from the Core creates authentic brands that emanate from the core of who an organization is.

The brand ecosystem model identifies components that, when operating as a whole, confirm the authenticity of the brand by aligning what is communicated by the organization with

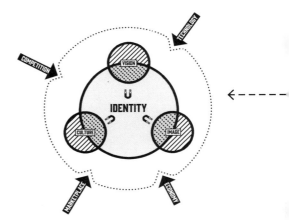

See Figure 7.1 for detailed graphic.

what is delivered. Think about your own personal experiences. You may first be attracted to a brand's story told through advertising and other forms of communication, but your loyalty is earned when the brand delivers what's been promised. If the organization continues to meet or exceed your expectations, not only does your trust in it (and its products or services) grow, you're also likely to tell everyone you know just how great it is.

As depicted in Figure 7.2, the positive reputation of an organization evolves and strengthens as various components of the brand ecosystem grow more cohesive over time. The result of this virtuous spiral is a reputation that reflects the highest intentions of the leadership. On the other hand, organizations unable to create this alignment spin into a vicious cycle that results in dysfunction of the organization and movement away

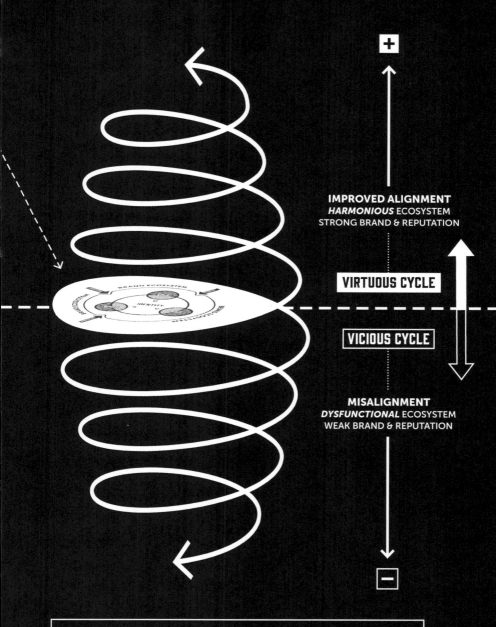

+

IMPROVED ALIGNMENT
HARMONIOUS ECOSYSTEM
STRONG BRAND & REPUTATION

VIRTUOUS CYCLE

VICIOUS CYCLE

MISALIGNMENT
DYSFUNCTIONAL ECOSYSTEM
WEAK BRAND & REPUTATION

—

Figure 7.2. Return on Reputation Virtuous/Vicious Cycle

from the leadership's vision. Thus, the goal of Branding from the Core is to create a virtuous cycle that builds reputations able to support the realization of the organization's vision by managing the cohesion between the elements of the brand ecosystem.

Brand Ecosystem Alignment as Strategy

Unlike traditional views of brand management as something controlled by a department and usually focused on the development of external images, the brand ecosystem offers a whole system view of brand management. This expands the brand management role to that of an integrated team of boundary-spanners who understand the nature of brands as ecosystems. This cross-functional team is tasked with creating relationships that people trust by managing cohesion between internal and external communications. In this context, communication is defined as the integration of what is heard, what is seen, and what is experienced.

The meaning people associate with a name is the brand. A brand is impacted in part by the story you tell and in part by the story others tell about you. The foundational premise of Branding from the Core is that brand development strategies must not *only* focus on telling a story that *you* have carefully crafted. This is true more today than ever before. While communications were once easily defined by words such as *internal* and *external*, we now grapple with a highly connected matrix in which the boundaries that were once so defined have blurred. This has intensified the need to embrace the importance of not only telling a story that's meaningful but also living that story through every person in your organization and every experience someone has with your organization. As Olins advised, every interaction matters, and every touch point offers a moment that speaks either the truth or the lie of the brand. Adopting the view of organizations as brand ecosystems offers a workable framework for dealing with this reality.

A branding strategy that produces the authenticity needed to compete in today's marketplace must choreograph a dynamic and integrated dance between the components of the ecosystem. If the components of the brand ecosystem become disconnected, organizations

> **EVERY TOUCH POINT OFFERS A MOMENT THAT SPEAKS EITHER THE TRUTH OR THE LIE OF THE BRAND.**

become dysfunctional unless efforts are made to bring these components into alignment. Misalignment often occurs when a new vision is introduced, when there's confusion about where the organization is going, when an organization has done a poor job telling its story, or when it fails to deliver on a story that's told. These misalignments produce a weak brand.

The Brand Ecosystem (see Figure 7.1) redefines brand management as organization strategy. The dotted areas in the model reflect the expression of the organization's identity narrative through the implementation of image development strategies and tactics, and brand experiences that are in line with the organization's vision. As such, they *affect* how the organization wants to be perceived. The areas depicted as diagonal lines in the model represent the *impressions* people have of the organization, in other words, the *effect* of the communication strategies. Successful brand development efforts produce tighter coupling between the expression of the organization's identity narrative and the impressions held by the marketplace. As these spheres gradually overlap, greater cohesion is forged between image, culture, and identity with the vision of the organization, thus, propelling the organization toward its envisioned future. The Brand Ecosystem provides a strategic framework for building reputations (see Virtuous Cycle Figure 7.2) that support the vision of the organization. On the following pages, we'll share examples of common gaps in The Brand Ecosystem that brand strategies should address.

IDENTITY–VISION GAP.

When a new vision is introduced that is significantly out of alignment with the existing identity of the organization, a new narrative must be introduced to bring the system into balance. This was the case at Interface when Ray Anderson introduced his new vision of Interface as a sustainable manufacturer. This idea was alien to the company's self-perception and to how Interface was viewed by the external marketplace. This lack of cohesion represents the most extreme of all of these scenarios, requiring the most time and energy to address, because it involves all components of the system.

VISION–CULTURE GAP.

This gap is evidenced when frustrations emerge among leaders because they feel members of the organization are not, or cannot, deliver on their aspirations for the company. This is often expressed by questions like, "Why can't we get everyone on the same page?" On the flip side, employees exhibit increased stress, frustration, and lack of motivation because they don't feel connected to the bigger goals of the organization. This may be because they don't understand the vision or don't feel connected to it. In most cases this also has residual effects on the image of the organization—unhappy employees will ultimately yield dissatisfied customers and in turn a negative image in the marketplace.

VISION-IMAGE GAP.

When the images held by the marketplace are disconnected from the aspirations of the leadership, it is difficult for the organization to move to the next level. This misalignment of perceptions results from the failure to deliver consistent, compelling communications that reinforce the desired image. This gap is usually expressed as, "we just aren't telling our story well," or "people don't understand who we are."

IMAGE-CULTURE GAP.

When the organization fails to deliver on the story told we say the culture is out of alignment. This is expressed as skepticism and distrust by those both inside and outside of the organization. Ensuring this alignment is important for all organizations, but is particularly important for organizations that want to position themselves as values-based organizations.

The Brand Transformation Journey explained in the next chapter can be used as a planned change intervention to realign the ecosystem in all of these situations. Successful implementation will create the authenticity and trust needed to build healthy organizations, strong brands, and respected reputations.

The following Spotlights feature both Martha D. Saunders, president of the University of West Florida, and Steve Hayes, executive director of Visit Pensacola, as they share their perspectives and provide examples of how they engaged their stakeholders in creating and supporting the development of their organization's brand. Both initiaives resulted in stronger alignment between the vision, identity, and culture of their organizations.

SPOTLIGHT #4

In January 2017, Martha D. Saunders became the sixth president of the University of West Florida (UWF). One of her first steps was to establish a vision statement to guide the strategic growth of the university. Having started her early academic career at UWF, she recognized the importance of strengthening the connection between the vision and culture of the campus.

> **The University of West Florida Vision Statement**
> **We are a spirited community of learners, launching the next generation of big thinkers who will change the world.**

Working with the UWF internal communications team, idgroup executed a storytelling initiative to communicate both the vision statement of the university as well as the impact professors are making on their students' lives and, in turn, how the university is impacting these research scholars.

The Power of Stories to Reinforce Culture

by Martha D. Saunders, *President, The University of West Florida*

By its very nature, college is a transformational experience. It is a rite of passage and, in truth, provides us with the first days of the rest of our lives as adults. We discover our professions there. Some of us meet our mates. We make memories that last a lifetime and we form lasting bonds.

Few of our college relationships are as influential as those between students and their teachers. At the University of West Florida, we leveraged those relationships by telling *their* stories. The results paid off as we focused on refining our brand. We called the campaign "Make Your Mark" and began by asking our top students two simple questions: "Who's your favorite teacher?" and "What makes him/her so special?"

We then asked the selected faculty two corresponding questions: "What attracted you to come to teach at our university?" and "What keeps you here?" We recorded the results, filmed videos of the faculty telling their own passionate, compelling stories, and launched a campaign that is tracking the evolution of our university. It has a life of its own and echoes our essential brand better than any professional scripter could do. The Make Your Mark campaign has defined the soul of our university. A student life administrator summed it up best: "For half a century UWF's only tradition has been to never be confined by tradition. I never want that to change."

The stories we gathered were shared across the campus and beyond into the community through an integrated campaign that included print ads, videos, and a landing page.

ABOUT

Martha D. Saunders
President, The University of West Florida

In her 30-plus years in higher education, Martha has served as a professor of communication, honors director, dean of arts & sciences, provost, chancellor, or president at universities in Florida, Georgia, Wisconsin, and Mississippi. Her area of academic expertise is in public relations and crisis communication for which she has won numerous awards, including two Public Relations Society of America's coveted Silver Anvils.

She earned her bachelor's degree in French from the University of Southern Mississippi, her master's degree in Journalism from the University of Georgia, and her doctorate in Communication Theory and Research from Florida State University.

Her philosophy of leadership parallels her philosophy of teaching: know your students, connect them to bigger things, and set a good example.

When she is not attending to university needs, Martha and her husband, Joe Bailey, can be found walking, shelling, gardening, kayaking, or fishing on her beloved Pensacola Beach.

UNIVERSITY *of* WEST FLORIDA

The University of West Florida (UWF) is tucked away in the beautiful corner of Northwest Florida. The campus, situated in 1,600 acres of unspoiled, natural woodlands, has over 13,000 students and offers over 70 undergraduate, graduate, and post-graduate degree programs.

"The University of West Florida gave me the biggest lab a researcher could ever ask for: 6,000 acres of public land and 19,000 acres of water along 52 miles of Gulf and bay shoreline. All at my fingertips."

ALEXIS JANOSIK, PH.D.
Assistant Professor • Department of Biology

UNIVERSITY *of* WEST FLORIDA

MAKE YOUR MARK

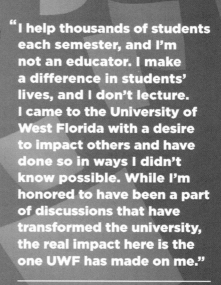

"I help thousands of students each semester, and I'm not an educator. I make a difference in students' lives, and I don't lecture. I came to the University of West Florida with a desire to impact others and have done so in ways I didn't know possible. While I'm honored to have been a part of discussions that have transformed the university, the real impact here is the one UWF has made on me."

 JOFFERY GAYMON, ED.D
Vice President • Enrollment and Student Affairs

UNIVERSITY *of* **WEST FLORIDA**

MAKE YOUR MARK

"**The University of West Florida believed in me and my passion for developing an undergraduate research program. Today, our chemistry scholars rank second in the nation, tied with Stanford, for most awarded scholarships.**"

KAREN S. MOLEK, PH.D.
*Administrative Fellow for Student Engagement • **Department of Chemistry***

UNIVERSITY *of* WEST FLORIDA

"At my old school,
I never interacted with
my students. I conducted
research and showed up
to lecture twice a week
to a class of hundreds.
I chose the University of
West Florida over Michigan
State because I wanted
to research, apply that
knowledge in the classroom,
and build meaningful
relationships with my
students."

SCOTT B. KELLER, PH.D
John C. Pace Distinguished
Business Professor • Department
of Marketing & Economics

UNIVERSITY *of* WEST FLORIDA

SPOTLIGHT #5

Visit Pensacola is responsible for the development and growth of the Pensacola Bay Area as a destination brand. When Steve Hayes took over the leadership reins in 2013, the organization needed significant restructuring to become more competitive in the marketplace. As Steve set forth planning the next stage of the organization's development, he wanted to hear ideas from the community about how to move Pensacola forward as a vacation destination. In the spirit of Steve's desire to engage community stakeholders, idgroup led Visit Pensacola through a first-ever strategic planning initiative for the community dubbed Destination 2020. By utilizing the Branding from the Core process, we engaged the people of the Pensacola community in creating a strategic plan to move the organization to the next level of success.

....

The Power of Community Dialogue
Destination 2020: Designing Our Future Together
by Steve Hayes, *President, Visit Pensacola, Inc.*

We began the Destination 2020 process with a question: *How do we rev-up tourism as an economic engine for our community?* We were guided by our desire to expand our focus beyond just attracting visitors, to creating a community where people want to visit *and* live.

The framework presented in this plan emerged from a nine-month research process. Central to this approach to planning was our commitment to engage a wide range of community stakeholder opinions, understanding relevant research about industry trends and current visitor behaviors, as well as the best practices in the destination marketing industry. More than 500 community members from all walks of life and from all areas of Escambia County participated in multiple dialogue sessions and surveys.

The result was the development of a vision and mission statement, clarity about the strengths and aspirations of the community, as well as some things that need work in order to become the best place to live, work, and play. All of the information gathered from the dialogue sessions was summarized into a comprehensive five-year strategic plan to guide the actions needed to realize the community's vision of the future we had created together.

At the end of the process, we shared the results of the work we did together during a celebratory event in which we applauded the uniqueness of our community and kicked off the implementation of the plan. Today, the Destination 2020 plan serves as a living document and continues to guide the development of Visit Pensacola.

Following the launch of the Destination 2020 strategic plan, *idgroup*—in collaboration with Showcase Pensacola— launched a new external branding and marketing campaign. Over the past four years, these efforts have resulted in a 48% increase in the numbers of visitors to the Pensacola area; 33% increase in visitor spending; and 30% increase in local taxes paid by visitors.

Information on the following pages is from the Destination 2020 Strategic Plan report.

Destination 2020: Designing Our Future Together is a community initiative led by Visit Pensacola that engages community members from Pensacola, Pensacola Beach, and Perdido Key in identifying opportunities to enhance our community and assets so we may continue to develop our potential as a great place to live and visit.

The goal of this plan was to answer the question, *"How do we rev-up tourism as an economic engine for our community?"* Data was gathered from multiple sources and analyzed to produce the findings and recommendations in this report.

Destination 2020 Strategic Plan

- O   Interviews With Government Leaders
- O   Research of Exemplar Communities
- O   Review of Local State Tourism Data
- O   Analysis of National and State Destination Marketing Trends
- O   Insight Meetings with the Visit Pensacola Strategic Planning Design Team
- O   Insights from Tourism Experts
- O   Community Dialogues
- O   Community Surveys

Mission

Lead. Connect. Collaborate. Communicate. Visit Pensacola supports the community vision of tourism by serving as the central body responsible for building tourism as an economic engine for our community.

In this role, Visit Pensacola functions to lead efforts directly related to the attraction and retention of tourists to our community. Visit Pensacola collaborates with other organizations with niche interests related to this mission. In addition, Visit Pensacola serves to connect others to various entities that impact development and infrastructure vital to supporting our community vision. We also facilitate communication among various groups to create an atmosphere of trust, engagement, and pride.

Vision

Tourism is a vital, highly valued, and strongly supported economic engine for our community.

Commitment to this vision has produced a better quality of life for residents, a preferred destination for visitors, and measurable economic results.

KICK-OFF DIALOGUE SESSION HELD AT THE HISTORIC PENSACOLA MUSEUM OF COMMERCE

THESE UNDERLYING THEMES WERE FURTHER DEFINED BY FIVE AREAS OF STRATEGIC FOCUS THAT PROVIDED A FRAMEWORK FOR ACTION:

- Increased economic impact of visitors
- Asset and product development
- Infrastructure and community development
- Community communication, collaboration, connections, and partnerships
- Evolving role of Visit Pensacola

7 DIALOGUE SESSIONS WERE HELD THROUGHOUT THE COMMUNITY

DESTINATION 2020 EVENT DAY

STEVE HAYES AND DON TRISTAN DE LUNA
CELEBRATING THE FOUNDING OF PENSACOLA

SAND ARTIST CHARLENE LANZEL, ILLUSTRATED PENSACOLA STORY

ABOUT

Steve Hayes
President of Visit Pensacola

Steve Hayes serves as the president of Visit Pensacola, Inc., the official destination marketing organization (DMO) for Pensacola, Pensacola Beach, and Perdido Key in Northwest Florida. As a DMO, Visit Pensacola's mission is to serve as the central body responsible for leading efforts directly related to the attraction and retention of visitors to the community. In 2015, Hayes and Visit Pensacola led a first-of-its-kind community initiative in Pensacola, dubbed "Destination 2020," that brought together the voices of businesses, elected officials, visitors, and citizen-taxpayers.

Prior to Visit Pensacola, Hayes served as the executive vice president of Visit Tampa Bay, where his contributions successfully secured Tampa Bay as the location for the 2012 Republican National Convention and Super Bowl XXXV in 2009. Hayes currently serves on the board of directors of United States Travel Association Destinations Council, as Chairman of the Florida Association of Destination Marketing Organizations, and is an active member of and contributor to Visit Florida and Destinations International.

Final Thoughts

Wally Olins' view of branding was on target, but the whole system view of branding requires an equally different framework for how we do branding. The brand ecosystem provides a new way to visualize organizations as brands. The ultimate goal of the Brand Transformation Journey, explained in the next chapter, is the choreographing of the ecosystem to support the development of a desired reputation. While you can't *control* your organization's reputation, perceptions created over time through the Branding from the Core methodology can influence it.

This view of branding holds that brands are shared stories created through dialogue with all your stakeholders. This includes all the groups that impact your success: customers, employees, investors, vendors, accountants, lawyers—everyone is part of your story.

The five stages of the Brand Transformation Journey are explained in the following chapter as a planned change process that results in transforming or strengthening organization brands from the inside out and outside in.

"People don't resist change. They resist being changed."

— Peter Senge

CHAPTER 8:
THE PROCESS:
THE BRAND TRANSFORMATION JOURNEY

This chapter addresses the need for organizations to effectively deal with increasingly skeptical audiences and the growing call from the marketplace for companies to demonstrate actions that prove their commitment to being good corporate citizens. These issues are addressed by creating organizations built on purpose and backed up by performance. The Branding from the Core transformation journey ensures authenticity by forging cohesion among the various components of the organization's brand ecosystem. This strengths-based stakeholder engagement process shifts an organization's one-dimensional view of branding—rooted in external messaging—into a rich, vibrant, multifaceted experience that has unparalleled impact on business results, organization members, communities, and the world.

The process builds on the foundations of positive organization studies—emphasizing the highly generative power of Appreciative Inquiry to transform *business-as-is* to *business as-it-can-be.*

Summary of the Relational Consequences of Appreciation (Ludema, Cooperrider, and Barrett, 2001)

> **1. Releases Positive Conversation Within the Organization:** *Unconditional positive questions ignite a virtual explosion of constructive conversations that refocus an organization's attention away from problems and toward hopeful, energizing possibilities.*
>
> **2. Builds an Ever-Expanding Web of Inclusion and Positive Relationships:** *An ever-increasing number of voices are included in conversations that highlight strengths, assets, hopes, and dreams. Respect, understanding, and strong relational bonds are formed.*
>
> **3. Creates Self-Reinforcing Learning Communities:** *As positive vocabularies multiply, people strengthen their capacity to put possibilities into practice. Organizational members learn increasingly sophisticated vocabularies for doing things in new ways.*
>
> **4. Bolsters Democracy and Self-Organizing:** *Appreciative self-organizing systems are marked by an epistemic stance of liberation, freedom, solidarity, social construction, and a deep appreciation for the miracle and mystery of organizational life.*
>
> **5. Provides a Reservoir of Strength and Unleashes a Positive Revolution of Change:** *The aim of appreciative inquiry is to discover the organization's "positive core," which provides continuity, strength, and stability in the face of turbulence and is also the source of energy for positive innovation and change.*

Three mantras of change management serve as inspiration for the process:

> » **People will defend and protect that which they help create,**
>
> » **The answers are in the room and the best answers aren't always found behind the biggest desks,**
>
> » **It is difficult to read the label from inside the bottle.**

First, people relish the opportunity to contribute to, and be part of, a solution. Because of their contribution, they are "bought into" the idea and will work to ensure its success. Conversely, people are more prone to resisting being used as an instrument for someone else's ideas, solutions, or answers. As a result, the likelihood that change initiatives will be successful increases with active participation from those who are contributing to the solution, and decreases when the people most affected by changes are left on the sidelines. Simply stated, people will defend and protect that which they help create. Branding from the Core rejects traditional top-down approaches that leave key players out of the process, and instead offers a more inclusive, lateral approach that engages all levels of the whole organization—from the smallest desks, to the corner office.

The Branding from the Core methodology acknowledges the second mantra: The answers are in the room, and the best answers aren't always found behind the biggest or most powerful desks. The most imaginative answers to almost any question can be found when we are willing to engage a cross section of people, from all corners of the organization, with different experiences and, therefore, different points of view.

Lastly, in some cases, additional thinking beyond the organization's purview may be required to shake things up, ignite new insights, and take the organization's views to new levels. The Branding from the Core methodology recognizes the third mantra by rejecting insular thinking. When we look outside the walls of the organization, we are able to unleash the shackles of what can be seen or imagined beyond the restrictions of "the way things have always been." Don't hesitate to look beyond the limitations of your organization's worldview to others who can shake up your thinking with unique ideas. For Interface, this type of openness to different perspectives proved to be one of the most valuable factors in its successful transformation. Early in the company's journey, founder Ray Anderson assembled a group of experts he called the Eco Dream Team; external people who were invited into the system. They served as advisors, partners, and new social referents; people who helped to usher in new ways of seeing things at Interface. Anderson described these people as "a group of advisors we pulled together to help us get our map straight." This team also served as valuable third-party validation to the world that Interface was the real deal.

Thus, the Brand Transformation Journey works to rally your team in defining solutions, creating buy-in at all levels of the organization, and inviting outside perspectives in helping to shape a more focused direction—your map—by shaping, sharing, and living the organization's brand identity narrative.

Shaping, Sharing, and Living the Brand

Transforming organizations into brands that matter begins by engaging key voices of the people who influence the success of organizations. Through this process we uncover and expand the characteristics typically used to describe strong brands—desirability, distinctiveness, and credibility—by adding responsibility to the list. Thus, responding to the call of today's conscious consumers who demand greater alignment with their values, this additional characteristic addresses the need for organizations to define a social contract and moral compass that balances what's good for both the organization and society.

- **DESIRABILITY:** What does the organization offer that is valuable to its audiences?

- **DISTINCTIVENESS:** What makes this organization stand out from the competition?

- **CREDIBILITY:** Why should people trust the organization?

- **RESPONSIBILITY:** How does this organization hold itself accountable to customers, employees, and the world?

This journey promises to create an organization that prospers because employees are proud to be a part of it, customers want to be connected with it, and the world benefits from it. Each organization's journey will be unique. But the final destination for all will be the strengthening of their desired brands.

The five stages of the Brand Transformation Journey introduced in the following section establish milestones along a path that ultimately leads to a cohesive brand ecosystem. The first four stages usually take around nine months to implement.

The fifth stage is an on-going, continuous improvement cycle that ensures the positive evolution of the brand toward a reputation that reflects the vision of the organization.

An Overview: Connecting Appreciative Inquiry to the Stages of the Transformation Journey

Figure 8.1 provides a view of the stages of the Brand Transformation Journey from immersion to evolution. The backbone of this process is based on the five phases of Appreciative Inquiry—Define, Discover, Dream, Design, and Destiny—with an additional sixth phase added to the Brand Transformation process: Develop. This sixth stage reflects a view of organization brands as dynamic and continuously evolving.

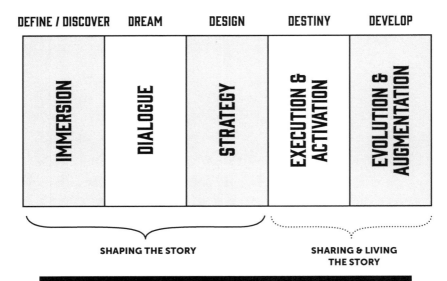

Figure 8.1. Stages of the Brand Transformation Journey

The following pages provide an overview that connects each stage of the Brand Transformation Journey: Immersion, Dialogue, Strategy, Execution, and Evolution to the phases of Appreciative Inquiry that were introduced in Chapter 6.

STAGE 1. IMMERSION / DISCOVER

Where are we? Organizations don't embark upon change without a compelling reason to do so. As mentioned earlier, change initiatives won't be successful without the leadership's commitment to the process. Motivations to embark upon the Brand Transformation Journey are often driven by perceived gaps in the brand ecosystem. While intuition or anecdotal information is frequently a catalyst for action, it is important to do the research needed to paint as clear a picture as possible of where the organization stands, relative to its goals and aspirations for the future. Translated from both the Define and Discover phase of Appreciative Inquiry, the Immersion stage represents the first step along the Transformation Journey. Here, we uncover the leadership's perspectives of the organization's current status and aspirational goals. The focus in this first stage is to bring situational awareness to the leadership team regarding the organization's current state and generate consensus around its potential and possibilities for the future, which together begin to shape and define the areas of inquiry that will be explored in the next stage: Dialogue / Dream.

STAGE 2. DIALOGUE / DREAM

Who are we and why do we matter? The Dream phase of
Appreciative Inquiry represents the second stage of the
Transformation Journey: Dialogue. Attention is focused inside
the organization by engaging a full range of people across
leadership and stakeholder dialogue sessions intended to uncover
their perspectives about the organization's Strengths, Aspirations,
Opportunities, and desired Results. These facilitated meetings
produce information and insights that are compiled and used
to create an organization identity platform, an identity narrative,
and areas of strategic focus, which will be further defined in
Stage 3 of the process, Strategy / Design.

STAGE 3. STRATEGY / DESIGN

Where are we going and how will we get there? In the Strategy
phase of the journey, plans are designed for repositioning and
realigning the brand ecosystem. The information uncovered in
the immersion and dialogue stages is combined, analyzed, and
translated into a strategic plan for both sharing the storylines
through formal communications and living the storylines
through customer and employee experiences. The Strategy stage
begins by identifying gaps in the ecosystem and opportunities
for strengthening the relationships between the entire system.
From here, we establish the objectives as strategic areas of focus
that define the priorities for the organization. Based on this
information, a strategic and tactical plan is developed to define

the actions, roles, and resources required to close the gaps and strengthen the system. With the plan in place, creative assets and performance improvement initiatives are developed that will be deployed in the next stage: Destiny / Execution.

STAGE 4. DESTINY / EXECUTION

Let's go. In the execution stage of the Brand Transformation Journey we set in motion the destiny of the organization. In this stage, both the creative image development assets and customer experience strategies created in Stage 3 are brought to life. This multi-pronged approach builds awareness, interest, and action through an integrated mix of multiple communication channels. While the role of external messaging is to move people to action, once moved, it is imperative to deliver *Moments of Truth* through customer experiences. Continuous delivery of these moments of truth at every interaction confirm the authenticity of formal messaging, thus supporting the successful movement of people from action, to satisfaction, to loyalty and, ultimately, to advocacy.

STAGE 5. DEVELOP / EVOLUTION

Let's grow. Successful transformation of organizations into brands that matter is a continuous process of strengthening the alignment of the ecosystem. This represents an expansion of Appreciative Inquiry's 5-D Model to a sixth stage, Develop, which translate to stage 5 of the Brand Transformation Journey: Evolution. In this stage, we continually monitor, develop, and adapt our strategy and tactics to maximize stronger alignment of the brand ecosystem. By elevating the role of brand development from a departmental initiative to the management of the whole organization as a dynamic brand ecosystem, we redefine branding as a process of continuously evolving the organization's reputation to reflect its highest aspirations.

Readiness for Change

I opened the book with an invitation to entrepreneurial thinkers and organizations to design and lead their organizations as brands that matter. I pause here to reinforce that a successful journey to this destination requires introspection about the organization's readiness for change. This is a critical—if not the most crucial prerequisite—to the success of the Branding from the Core process. Without a willingness and readiness for change, no manner of hard work, determination, or good intentions will help leaders achieve the full potential this process offers. The force field analysis on the following page provides a framework for this conversation among the leadership.

Motivations for Change

Leadership teams may find the force field analysis model (Figure 8.2) helpful in guiding discussion about readiness for change. This was developed by social psychologist Kurt Lewin to help organizations understand forces that either drive people toward or against a decision to change. According to Lewin (1948), "To bring about any change, the balance between the forces which maintain the social self-regulation at a given level has to be upset." Using the force field analysis framework you can create a list of factors either supporting change or opposing change to reflect the strength of the forces. Once the leadership team has worked through this conversation, is clear about the motivations for change, and commits to the process, the real work can begin.

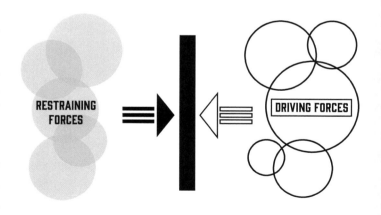

RESTRAINING FORCES

DRIVING FORCES

Figure 8.2. Force Field Analysis (Adapted from Lewin 1948)

STAGE 1

IMMERSION

Where are we?

IMMERSION   DIALOGUE   STRATEGY   EXECUTION   EVOLUTION

STAGE 1 · IMMERSION
WHERE ARE WE?

In this stage, primary and secondary research is gathered to uncover the organization's current situation. Informal discussions are held with the leadership team around their insights and impressions. In addition, various sources are reviewed to answer the questions on the following pages. The insights gained from this phase generate the Immersion Report, which helps to shape the questions that will be asked in the Dialogue phase (leadership and organizational).

Sample questions explored in the Immersion Stage

» Who are your customers/audiences? What do they care about? What needs do they have, and how are you meeting those needs?

» Through what methods and channels do your customers engage with you?

» Who are your competitors? What are their strengths?

» What trends are happening within the industry that you need to be aware of?

» What are the constraints or opportunities of the current economic climate?

» What is the story you're currently telling?

- » Are you delivering what you promise to customers and employees?

- » How are you currently perceived by your stakeholders?

- » How do you want to be perceived?

- » Are you attracting loyal customers and the best and brightest employees?

- » Are your employees connected with the organization's mission and values?

- » What are your biggest perceived pain points that are keeping you from achieving success?

The Immersion Report reflects the leadership's collective insights:

1. Current situation around operational context of the organization:

    - » What are the wants, needs, desires of consumers/ marketplace?

    - » Where do we stand relative to the competition?

    - » What are the economic and financial factors that are impacting us?

2. What are the perceived gaps in the brand ecosystem?

3. Why do we need to change? What are the challenges to change? What are the benefits of change?

STAGE 2

DIALOGUE

Who are we and why do we matter?

WHO ARE WE AND WHY DO WE MATTER?

The Dialogue Phase of the Transformation Journey is split into two parts: The Leadership Dialogue session, and the Stakeholder Dialogue session. Both dialogue sessions contribute to shaping the brand's identity platform, brand narrative, and areas of strategic focus. This information is then collected, analyzed and drafted into a comprehensive findings report which will be translated in the third stage into strategies for sharing and living the story.

Leadership Dialogue Session

Information gathered during the Immersion Stage is used to shape questions to be explored during the Leadership Dialogue. This gathering of the leadership team provides time for reflection and discussion about opportunities to build upon current strengths toward an envisioned future.

Conversations during this session begin to uncover ideas that will shape a collective vision for the organization's future, a path toward this destination, and the results of successfully arriving at defined milestones along the way. In this session the leadership team has the opportunity to reflect upon and share their perspectives in a safe, open, and supportive environment.

Within Branding from the Core, the SOAR framework (see Figure 8.3) guides the development of questions asked during the Leadership Dialogue session. These questions uncover the areas of strategic focus in the final plan, and the information gained, along with other research, informs the questions that will be asked in the Stakeholder Dialogue session.

Leadership Dialogue Findings Report

Information uncovered in the Leadership Dialogue session is analyzed and synthesized to create a findings report. This report identifies key composite themes that are molded into a summary analysis of each of the questions asked during the dialogue session. The questions focus on identifying areas of strategic focus, the organization's social contract and moral compass, and leadership perspectives about the current alignment of the brand ecosystem. This analysis is reviewed with leadership to confirm accuracy of information, and to ensure nothing was lost in the translation and trascription of the data. Once leadership has provided confirmation of accuracy, the report can be used in the development of questions for the Stakeholder Dialogue session.

The SOAR Strategic Framework

This strategic framework, developed by Jacqueline Stavros and Gina Hinrichs (2009) and described in *The Thin Book of SOAR: Building Strengths-Based Strategy*, flips the traditional analysis of an organization's strategic position from strengths, weaknesses or problems, opportunities, and threats (SWOT/ SPOT) to strengths, opportunities, aspirations, and results (SOAR). Threats, weaknesses, or problems are not ignored, but they're reframed through the lens of "what we want more of."

SOAR applies an Appreciative Inquiry philosophy to strategic conversations, engaging all levels and functional areas of an organization, while SWOT is typically a top-down approach. When using a SOAR analysis to develop branding strategy, the basic questions are framed around four areas of inquiry as defined by Stavros and Hinrichs (see Figure 8.3).

S = Strengths: What an organization is doing really well, including its assets, capabilities, and greatest accomplishments.

O = Opportunities: External circumstances that could improve profits, unmet customer needs, threats, or weaknesses reframed into possibilities.

A = Aspirations: What the organization can be; what the organization desires to be known for.

R = Results: The tangible, measurable items that will indicate when the goals and aspirations have been achieved.

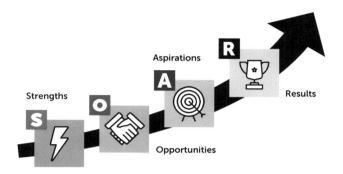

Figure 8.3. The SOAR Strategic Framework (Stavros and Hinrichs 2009)

Outcomes of the Leadership Dialogue Session

» SOAR Strategic Areas of Focus: Your strengths, opportunities, aspirations, and desired results.

» Social Contract Statement: How do you define your responsibility to your employees, your customers, and the world?

» Moral Compass Statement: How do you want your values to define the behaviors of your organization?

» Brand Ecosystem Assessment: What are the perceived gaps or weaknesses between your current image, culture, and vision?

Stakeholder Dialogue Session

In the second part of the Dialogue phase, we conduct the Stakeholder Dialogue session with questions aimed at expanding the perspectives shared in the Leadership Dialogue session. The Stakeholder Dialogue session brings together various voices from both inside and outside the organization. It is attended by key stakeholders—representative voices of *all* who can impact the success of your organization. Those who attended the Leadership Dialogue session should also attend this session. The value of the stakeholder dialogue session is found not only in uncovering information needed to shape the identity narrative and strategy, but also in what the participants learn from one another. By elevating the feelings of community among the attendees, seeds for collective action are planted. In many ways, the Stakeholder Dialogue session serves as a team-building exercise that invites important stakeholder groups (both inside and outside the organization) to contribute toward the development of the brand, to build on leadership's vision, and to connect on a deeper level with the organization's mission and values.

Throughout the day participants take part in exercises designed to uncover the core strengths of the organization, what it is doing well, as well as opportunities to achieve its aspirations for the future. We often explain the dialogues as similar to archeological digs, the goal being to unearth what, at the core, makes the organization great. Specifically, participants are asked to explore why this organization is a brand that matters to customers, employees, and the world. As a reminder, brands that matter are companies we love to love. They share core characteristics of desirability, credibility, distinctiveness, and responsibility. All questions in this dialogue are designed to focus attention on what's working while exploring opportunities to build on these characteristics. Topics are shaped into questions that tap into the imagination of participants to uncover the potential for the organization to reach new heights of vitality, health, and performance. The following pages offer a sample agenda and topics that are most often addressed and some examples of outcomes that were achieved for *idgroup* client Inspera Health.

Sample Stakeholder Dialogue Agenda

Below is a sample agenda of a typical one-day stakeholder dialogue session. Based on the goals of the organization and number of participants, dialogues may also be multi-day retreats. At *idgroup* we have conducted sessions ranging from six people to several hundred. During the session(s) participants are navigated through a series of activities intended to mine perspectives from stakeholders. The activities during the session are generative, each new activity building off the previous one. As such, it is important to have participants who will remain throughout the entire length of the session.

8:00	Gathering & Breakfast
8:45 - 9:30	Introduction and Opening Activities
9:30 - 10:30	**Activity 1:** Learning from Our Successes
10:30 - 11:30	**Activity 2:** Mapping Our Positive Core
11:30 - 12:30	**Activity 3:** Positive Core Report
	LUNCH
1:00 - 2:00	**Activity 4:** Envisioning Our Future Together
2:00 - 3:00	**Activity 5:** Development of Presentation to the Group
3:00 - 3:30	**Activity 6:** Presentation of Creative Expressions
3:30 - 3:45	Debrief Questions
3:45 - 4:00	Closing Comments/Adjourn

Stakeholder Dialogue Workbook

The following pages outline both the day's activities and sample questions used during the stakeholder dialogue session. The workbook is framed within the theme of "Celebrating our Past, Designing our Future Together." Activities in the morning session are focused on uncovering the strengths of the organization and learning from our successes. The activities in the afternoon session build on these strengths to envision possibilities for the future.

Activity 1: Learning from Our Successes

Purpose: This exercise has been designed to ensure that key voices in the organization are heard. The goal is to learn from our successes, uncover collective strengths, discover components of the organization's identity, and define a collective vision of our future.

Directions for Participants:

» Select an interview partner from your table.

» Interview your partner using the interview guide on the following pages.

» Everyone should answer all of the questions. Take turns answering questions before moving on to the next.

» Encourage your partner to tell his/her stories. Use active listening skills and positive encouragement to facilitate rich conversations.

» Take good notes during the conversation. Be prepared to share your interview partner's perspectives during large group discussion.

Sample Areas of Inquiry:

» **Attractors:** What attracted you to this organization and why do you remain associated with the organization?

» **Peak Experiences:** Stories of times when you have been most proud to be associated with this organization and why these examples stand out for you.

» **Impact:** What is the greatest difference we currently make to our employees, customers, and the world, beyond the products and services we offer?

» **Key Audiences:** Who is your tribe? What is important to this group?

» **Persona:** How is the organization currently perceived vs. how would it like to be perceived?

» **Value Proposition:** What makes this organization more desirable to your tribe than others?

» **Differentiation:** How would you complete this statement: "We are _____, they are not"?

» **Critical Path:** What are the most immediate actions that, if taken, would move this organization to the next level of success?

Activity 2: Mapping Our Positive Core

Purpose: As a table, discuss what you've uncovered from your interviews and record common themes from your conversations.

Directions for Participants:

» Select a recorder, timekeeper, and reporter for the table.

» Introduce your interview partner to the table. After everyone has been introduced, continue by sharing highlights from each question. The group should note key themes/ideas from each question and capture these ideas on the flip charts provided at each table as members share information from their interviews. What commonalities are you hearing as you listen to each other? Select one high-point story to share with the larger group.

Directions for Facilitator: Facilitate the completion of the activity among the partner groups, answer questions that arise from participants, and keep your participants on time.

Activity 3: Positive Core Report (facilitated activity)

Purpose: Each table shares insights with the others in the room.

Directions for Participants: Your table reporter will introduce the members of your table and present the key themes captured for each question. As you listen to the stories shared by the other tables, take note of any key ideas you feel are important.

Directions for Facilitator: The role of the facilitator is to encourage sharing of stories for each question, from each table.

Activity 4: Envisioning Our Future Together

Purpose: Great organizations are able to build on their core strengths while moving in the direction of their dreams and aspirations.

Directions for Participants: Reflect on your answers to all that you've heard here today. In your groups, discuss your wishes and visions for the future. Record on the flip charts the themes that you seem to share in common from your discussions. Follow the instructions as provided on the worksheets.

Directions for Facilitator: Facilitate the completion of the activity among table groups, answer questions that arise from participants, and keep your participants on time.

Sample Areas of Inquiry:

» **Envisioning:** Imagine we are sitting here years from now. It is the year 2030—we are in this room, reflecting on the success of this organization. It has been wildly successful and exceeded your greatest hopes and dreams. We have built an image in the marketplace, and delivered an experience to the community that aligns with the reputation we desired. Tell me about what has been accomplished. Take a few moments as a group and discuss these questions together.

As you talk through your answers, capture key themes on the flip charts provided.
- What are the successes we are most proud of?
- What are people in the community saying about us?
- What impact have we made on the community and/or society?

Please be specific.

» **Reputation Statement**: Building on your discussion, create an aspirational reputation statement that captures your vision of the reputation you've successfully built and maintained in 2330, and the critical success factors that helped you achieve this success. On your flip charts, complete the following sentence and provide the steps taken to achieve this vision.

In 2030 our organization is known as:

» **Actions:** What key actions did leadership take that moved this organization to the next level of success?

» **Visual Identity:** Name & Logo: Review the company logo. Does the current name and logo (symbol, colors, etc.) reflect the reputation you've defined as a group?

Would you make any changes to create better alignment with the reputation you've built in 2030? If so, what changes, adjustments, additions, or modifications would you make?

Activity 5: Development of Presentation to the Group

Directions for Participants: At your table groups, create a 5–7 minute creative presentation that reflects the organization as you have envisioned.

Include the following information in your presentation:
1. Aspirational Brand Reputation Statement
2. Key Successes
3. Strategic Areas of Focus and Action Items for reaching this vision
4. Modifications or adjustments you would make to the Name and Logo that better align with the organization as you have envisioned it.

Activity 6: Presentation of Creative Expressions

Directions for Participants: Each team will have 5–7 minutes to share their presentation.

Directions for Facilitator: Encourage the sharing of each group's presentation. Reflect back to the audience any key themes you're hearing throughout the presentations.

Core Brand Report

The information gathered during the Stakeholder Dialogue session is combined with the data from the Leadership Dialogue session. This composite view of both the leadership and stakeholder perspectives is then analyzed by researchers using thematic analysis, a qualitative research method used to find patterns in data. The combination of key themes from both dialogue sessions reflects the collective understanding about "who we are" (identity) and "where we want to go" (vision) and some ideas of what is needed to get from here to there.

From these themes, a Core Brand Report is created reflecting the synthesis of Leadership and Stakeholder perspectives. This includes the Provocative Proposition Statement, Organization Creed, and Critical Path (also called the Areas of Strategic Focus).

Provocative Proposition: A provocative proposition is a statement about the future of your organization (vision and reputation). It should be inspirational, imaginative, and daring. It should capture your passions in a way that clearly and concisely conveys the common vision of the future for your organization. Simply, this statement answers the question, "Where do we want to go?" while articulating the dreams and hopes for how you want your organization to be perceived.

Organization Creed: A set of beliefs that guides decisions and behaviors (reflecting your moral compass and social contract commitments). This is a declaration of your organization's core purpose. A carefully crafted creed answers the question, "Why do we exist?"

Critical Path: These areas of focus define high-level categories of what is needed to realize the provocative proposition while living the organization creed. These areas are defined from insights gathered about the core strengths, opportunities, aspirations, and desired results. The critical path should clarify the gaps in the ecosystem. Actions needed to close these gaps are defined in Phase 3.

STAGE 3

STRATEGY

*Where are we going
and how will we get there?*

STAGE 3 · STRATEGY
WHERE ARE WE GOING AND HOW WILL WE GET THERE?

In Stage 3 of the Brand Transformation Journey, we begin translating the intentions expressed in the Core Brand Report. Much like the Dialogue phase, the Strategy phase also has two parts: The first being the planning and development of the identity platform, brand narrative, and strategic areas of focus as informed by the Core Brand Report. The second part is the actual creation of assets, plans, and tactics that support the strategies approved by Leadership. Both parts of this stage combine to form the brand development map, which outlines actions required to move your organization toward its aspirations for the future by aligning the components of the brand ecosystem. By closing gaps and strengthening the brand ecosystem, we create the cohesion of expectations and experiences necessary to build trust and authenticity.

Developing the Brand Identity Platform

Recall the areas of inquiry used as part of the Stakeholder Dialogue session? The answers to those questions—with the inclusion of leadership's perspectives—are directly translated into the components of the brand identity platform. The brand identity platform is an expression of your organization's self-perception and specifically, what makes this organization desirable, distinctive, credible, and responsible. It responds to key questions in relation to the competition and the target audiences—*who we are, what we do, what makes us different,* and *why do we matter?* This information provides a cohesive and collective foundation of all communication. It's helpful to think about the platform as storylines—expressions of how the organization wants to be perceived. These storylines will be expressed throughout an organization's communications—internal and external—visual, verbal, and experiential.

THE PLATFORM INCLUDES:

» **Strengths:** What makes this organization great? What do we do really well?

» **Values:** Expressed as guiding principles of the organization.

» **Differentiated Value Proposition:** Captures the key reasons why your target audience chooses you over your competition. Includes functional and emotional motivators.

» **Persona:** Organizations, like people, have personalities. The persona captures the organization's face to the world: how it looks, acts, and speaks. This informs all visual and verbal communications.

» **Archetype*****:** Reflects the core motivations of the organization expressed in terms of one or a combination of the 12 archetypes.

···

*The work of Carol S. Pearson, Ph.D., offers excellent insight into archetypical storytelling applied to organization behavior.

» **Promise:** Defined as the sweet spot of branding. It lives at the intersection of the core identity of the organization and what is important to its audience.

» **Position:** Defines where the organization fits within its competitive landscape.

Drafting the Brand Identity Narrative

Organizations don't just tell stories; they *are* stories—and stories have power. Stories surround us. They are what we relate to. We watch movies and go to plays and performances. Songs are stories. We read books and poems. Even the nightly news consists of stories that unfold in real time. We share memories and document stories through film and photos. Everything we do involves story. Yet in business, the concept of an organization's story isn't seen as a powerful tool for connecting with audiences and stakeholders. The identity narrative, which lives at the heart of Branding from the Core, is the internal story that creates collective meaning for the diverse collection of people we define as organizations.

The identity narrative serves as the glue for your organization's formal communications, both internally and externally. It serves as a guiding light for the development of systems and processes that create *moments of truth*. We bring the narrative to life through the interactions people have with your organization.

It's important to note the nuanced difference between identity narrative and brand story. An identity narrative captures key storylines that define how the organization wants to be perceived, while the brand story is a co-constructed story that incorporates the perspectives and views of those outside of the organization. Thus, the identity narrative represents the intentions of the organization, while the brand story is the result of branding efforts.

The identity narrative weaves the components of the identity platform into the organization's story. The narrative captures accomplishments of the past and the greatest hopes for the future of the institution. As such, it is part celebration and part aspiration—a story that is in the process of "becoming" reality. It is used to inspire marketing communication materials, as well as internal performance.

To draft an organization's internal identity narrative, we turn to both the Core Brand Report and the Brand Identity Platform for inspiration. The elements in both the Core Brand Report and Brand Identity Platform serve as the beginning storylines. The Brand Identity Narrative takes these individual storylines and weaves them into one cohesive story—a creative expression written as a narrative that is used to inform all the organization's communications: internally and externally—visual, verbal, and experiential.

AN IDENTITY NARRATIVE CAPTURES KEY STORYLINES THAT DEFINE HOW THE ORGANIZATION WANTS TO BE PERCEIVED, WHILE THE BRAND STORY IS A CO-CONSTRUCTED STORY THAT INCORPORATES THE PERSPECTIVES AND VIEWS OF THOSE OUTSIDE OF THE ORGANIZATION.

The identity narrative can be used in many ways: as a tool to ensure that all the creative assets reflect the feelings captured in the narrative, as inspiration for your creative design teams as they produce campaigns and marketing messaging, to inspire employees through their performance to deliver on the narrative, and for recruitment of employees who resonate with the soul of the narrative.

Expressing the Brand Identity Narrative

Once the Brand Identity Narrative is written, we begin the second part of the Strategy phase. In this part, we further define the strategy and tactics, and develop the creative assets that translate the narrative into initiatives and interventions. The goal here is to align our Brand Ecosystem and move customers through the Brand Engagement Continuum, mentioned in the next stage. Expressing the brand is where we begin to walk our talk through the alignment of what our visual and verbal assets promise, and what we deliver—*Moments of Truth* that build trust, loyalty, and advocacy.

Expressing the Identity Narrative Through Image Development

By taking the information from both the Brand Identity Platform and the Brand Identity Narrative, we start to shape the visual and verbal components of our brand's messaging. The Identity-Image Development Map (Figure 8.4) illustrates the major components that will serve as the guiding star for all visual, verbal, and written communication from your brand. It may be helpful to think of the elements of the Identity-Image Development Map as the creative brief for every piece of communication put out to the marketplace: television spots, print advertisements, posters, social media posts, etc., as well as the key messages for any and all image development assets.

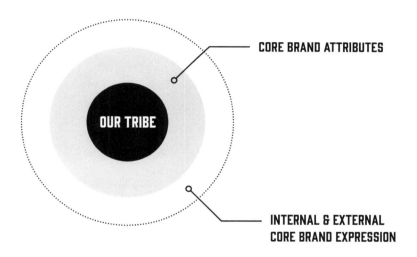

Figure 8.4. Identity-Image-Culture Map

OUR TRIBE.

The tribe lives at the center of this model because all organization brands exist in relationship to their audience. It's important to keep the wants, needs, and desires of the audience central to all communication efforts.

DEFINING THE TRIBE.

» Create a persona that represents a composite of your customers.

» Create a persona that represents your ideal employee.

CORE BRAND ATTRIBUTES.
Written from the perspective of your audience.

» Desirable (Why do they care about you?)

» Distinctive (Why are you different from their other choices?)

» Credible (Why should they trust you?)

» Responsible (What impact are you having beyond your offering?)

CORE BRAND EXPRESSIONS.
How will your organization express its identity to the world? This map reflects the desired perceptions of the organization as a brand.

» How do you look? (visual brand)

» How do you feel? (emotional attributes)

» How do you talk? (voice and tone, visual and verbal)

» How do you act? (experience)

Expressing the Identity Narrative Through Performance

Just as the Identity-Image-Culture Map frames the visual and verbal communications of our brand, it also shapes the behavioral methods for every touch point and the desired experiences that create *Moments of Truth* for our customers and employees. For instance, if we follow the path of a patient of a physician's office, the experience map would likely include: interaction with marketing communication efforts, initial phone call, appointment scheduling process, external office appearance, internal office appearance, check-in process, touch points throughout the appointment process, checkout, and follow-up communication.

This visual map brings the brand narrative to life at every corner of the office. We recommend it be created in conjunction with the employees expected to deliver the experience. The map identifies interactions that shape the customer perceptions and defines specific performance expectations at those touch points. These are the moments of truth that confirm (or reject) your identity narrative, and thus define the authenticity of the brand.

STAGE 4

EXECUTION

Let's go.

STAGE 4 · EXECUTION
LET'S GO.

To this point the focus of the journey has been on shaping the story and translating the story through the way the organization looks and acts. Now it's time to share that story with the world. I liken the first three stages of the Brand Transformation Journey to a makeover that ensures the visual expression of the organization is in line with the core of who it believes it is. In this stage, authenticity and relevancy are built by sharing and living the story through executing the plan that activates the brand through our visual, verbal, and behavioral communications. It's here that we ensure the story created during the Immersion, Dialogue, and Strategy phases is both shared and lived. In this stage, your brand engagement plan is executed through the brand continuum, which defines the stages of engagement that ultimately result in building brand advocates.

Brand Engagement Continuum

The visual representation of the brand continuum (see Figure 8.5 on the following page) reflects both telling your story and living your story. It acts as a framework to help you develop an action plan for creating expectations that resonate with audiences that are important to your organization's success, creating awareness and then interest that moves people to take action to engage with your organization. In the latter part of the continuum, performance standards define experiences that are consistent with the expectations created. The goal is for people who interact with your organization to move from satisfaction to loyalty, and ultimately to brand advocacy. This action plan is developed as part of your brand engagement plan, and it identifies tactics at each of the stages, along with leaders, metrics, and timelines for action.

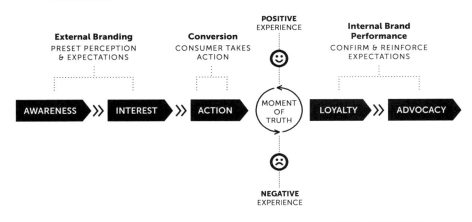

Figure 8.5. The Brand Continuum

SETTING EXPECTATIONS. People can't buy what they don't know about, and they won't buy what they don't have a compelling reason to buy. Branding from the Core responds to both of these truths. External brand communication, using the assets created in the strategy stage, builds awareness and interest and motivates people to take action. This means that they pick up the phone, go to a website, walk through your door, or in some other way engage with your organization. They do this because they saw a creative ad, or a video on YouTube, which tapped into feelings that moved them to take action. A lot of money is spent on various forms of communication designed to convince people to choose X over Y. Branding communication achieves this through emotional messaging that's designed to connect with the deeper motivations of the people you have identified as your audience. Going back to the sweet spot of branding (see Figure 4.1), brand communications are designed to create these associations. But the initial connections made through creative communications are only the beginning.

DESIGNING CUSTOMER EXPERIENCE STANDARDS. What's crucial to developing the trust required to build brand advocates is the ability of your organization to deliver on the sizzle created: Moments of Truth. Building trust begins by building satisfaction. This is measured using surveys and focus groups, or by simply asking the customer, *How are we doing?* Repeat business is also a measure of satisfaction. But satisfaction is thin ice—how many times have you been satisfied, but decided to move on to the next great hairdresser, physician, or restaurant anyway? The goal of Branding from the Core is to build brand-loyal communities. Your success is measured in terms of *loyalty*, which means a relationship that's not easily shaken, and *advocacy*, defined by the willingness of a person to stake his or her reputation on recommending you to others.

Setting appropriate performance standards ensures that your brand is lived throughout your organization. These standards are created by engaging employees in choreographing consistent and positive customer experiences, impressing people who interact with the organization at all touch points. This includes both on-ground and online experiences. Thus, building satisfaction, loyalty, and advocacy is all about delivering on the expectations that have been created in the first stages of the branding continuum. It is vital for your employee teams to be involved in defining these standards and in identifying ways to ensure consistent implementation and continuous improvement.

STAGE 5

EVOLUTION

Let's grow.

LET'S GROW.

Making adjustments along the journey ensures that the path you're on will take you to your desired destination. Thus, a key to sustaining success as a brand that matters is embedding continuous improvement and organization learning into your culture. This on-going process reflects a willingness to always be open to ways of strengthening the relationship with stakeholders, inside and outside of the organization. Becoming a learning organization by embedding the experiential learning (Figure 8.6) into the organization's systems and processes will ensure continuous improvement becomes a defining characteristic of the organization's culture. This is critical to maintaining the relevancy and credibility of the brand.

One model you may find helpful in guiding the development of a learning culture was developed in the early 1970s by David Kolb and Ron Fry. The cycle creates learning through experiences that progress from concrete experiences, reflections, conceptualization, and experimentation. This process is valuable as a process for reviewing and adjusting brand development strategies.

1. **CONCRETE EXPERIENCE:** A new experience is encountered, or an existing experience is reinterpreted.
2. **REFLECTIVE OBSERVATION:** Insights are gained from the new experience. It's important to note any inconsistencies between the experience and the understanding of it.
3. **ABSTRACT CONCEPTUALIZATION:** The reflective observation gives rise to a new idea or a modification of an existing idea.
4. **ACTIVE EXPERIMENTATION:** The learner applies new insights to the world to see what results.

CONCRETE EXPERIENCE
(doing / having
an experience)

ACTIVE EXPERIMENTATION
(playing / trying out what
you have learned)

REFLECTIVE OBSERVATION
(reviewing / reflective
on the experience)

**ABSTRACT
CONCEPTUALIZATION**
(concluding / learning
from the experience)

Figure 8.6. The Experiential Learning Cycle (Kolb and Fry 1974)

The key to organization learning is to give people permission to act on challenges they encounter. It's important to maintain an appreciative inquiry perspective in framing and exploring questions about how to deal with challenges. Instead of asking why something isn't working, reframe the issue in terms of

THE KEY TO
ORGANIZATION
LEARNING IS **TO
GIVE PEOPLE
PERMISSION
TO ACT ON
CHALLENGES
THEY ENCOUNTER.**

possibility. Once the question is posed, give people in your organization the freedom to engage team members in meeting the challenges by finding opportunities for improvement, asking:

1. What are we doing well? (Discover)
2. What do we think we can do better? (Dream)
3. How can we make what we imagine happen? (Design)
4. How do we implement those ideas? (Destiny)

Once implemented, the solution to your challenge should be reviewed to determine if additional tweaking is needed or if what was implemented is solid enough to stabilize the situation. If you embed this way of thinking into the way your organization does things, you'll find that employees remain engaged and will constantly look for ways to improve the performance of your organization.

The following actions should be built into your organization learning program to enhance the engagement, trust, and pride of your organization's members:

ACTION 1 | **BE TRANSPARENT ABOUT RESULTS.**

Create a method for reporting the defined actions and their results in your brand development strategy. Establish regular reporting processes and engage employees in finding new opportunities to reach the goals that have been set.

ACTION 2 | **LISTEN. LEARN. ACT.**

It's important to build time into your organization's calendar for formal and informal meetings that place your customer experience standards and brand continuum at the center of your conversation. You need to ask: *What's working? What needs to change? Are we still committed to this?* This keeps the strategic plan alive as opposed to it sitting somewhere on the shelf until the next yearly planning meeting. Another important aspect of this action is to stay connected with what's happening outside the organization since any external shifts may impact the plan.

ACTION 3 | **CONTINUE TO PUSH EXCELLENCE THROUGH EDUCATION.**

Investing in people results in one of the highest ROIs possible. New ideas keep organizations innovating. Inspire your team with speakers, webinars, podcasts, or other resources, but don't overlook the skills, knowledge, and inspiration that the people in your own organization can share. Informal lunch-and-learns, where people in the organization can share best practices or simply engage in conversations, offer multiple advantages, especially elevating people's esteem.

ACTION 4 | **ENJOY THE JOURNEY AND CELEBRATE SUCCESS.**

Transforming organizations to be brands that matter is a journey. There will be ups and downs, so it's important to celebrate the successes along the way. One of my favorite lines from a Jimmy Buffett song reflects the fast-forward world we live in: "I took off last week to try to remember the entire year." An important role of leadership is to build-in moments of reflection and celebration—that is, time for everyone on the team to reconnect to purpose and to celebrate the difference they are making and the legacy they are leaving. Taking time to recognize successes is something most of us fail to do. We tend to pull everyone together to handle the challenges, but only give a passing nod to our victories.

Recognizing success should not be limited to annual meetings or employee reviews. Find the time to pause, reflect, and recognize moments when your team has contributed to clients, to the community, or to each other. People need to be loved and appreciated, so a real-time thank you goes a long way in building job satisfaction and commitment.

THE INSPERA HEALTH TRANSFORMATION JOURNEY

The following pages share outcomes of
the Branding from the Core process
through the experience of one of our
clients, Inspera Health.

Who is Inspera Health?

The focus of Inspera Heath is on improving the quality of life for people living with multiple chronic health conditions. The innovative model developed by the company utilizes an integrated, multi-disciplinary approach that leverages intrinsic coaching principles for igniting real and lasting change. This change is acheived by combining exercise, nutrition, and counseling with other forms of alternative healthcare, such as yoga, massage, and acupuncture to reach the health objectives of its clients. By improving the quality of life of people, the company also seeks to improve the productivity of people in their work environments, and to reduce the high utilization of healthcare costs for self-insured organizations.

Inspera's Readiness for Change

Lee Murphy, CEO of Inspera Health (previously known as Integrated Case Management L3C), contacted *idgroup* because he felt his organization needed to pause and reflect upon where they were and where they wanted to go. While the company was successful since its inception, Lee felt it was ready for the next level. After conversations with Lee and the leadership team about the Branding from the Core approach, they felt this would be a good process to help them meet their objectives. Through a series of conversations with his leadership team, the decision was made that they were ready, willing, and able to take this next step.

The first step in the journey was to work with Lee to create a Design Team to collaborate with the *idgroup* team throughout the stages of the brand transformation process: Immersion, Dialogue, Strategy, and Execution. A design team is a small working group that serves as the steering committee throughout the Brand Transformation Journey. The Design Team comprises various key leaders or their representatives who play a major role in the success and outcome of this initiative. In effect, this design committee acts as the champions of the transformation journey.

With the Design Team in place, we began our journey that resulted in the transformation of Integrated Case Management LC3 into Inspera Health.

Inspera Health Dialogues

Findings from the Leadership Dialogue were used to inform the questions that were asked during the stakeholder dialogue session. The design team worked with *idgroup* to outline key topics for the stakeholder session and to determine the voices that needed to be included in the dialogue sessions. The final list included about 60 participants consisting of a mix of employees, clients, participants, and providers.

The group came together for an eight-hour session dubbed: Celebrating our Past, Designing our Future, Together. The dialogue session was divided into five exercises designed to inspire ideas and uncover insights about how the company can best reach its goals. The process is very generative as each exercise builds upon the previous one. These exercises were designed to uncover the core strengths of the organization, what it was doing well, and opportunities to achieve its aspirations for the future.

Questions throughout the day focused on uncovering the participant's perspectives about: core strengths of the organization, stakeholder perceptions, value proposition and differentiation, personality, core values, exemplars of best practices, greatest opportunities to reach the next level of success, development of a provocative proposition statement for the future of the organization, and insights about the current name and logo.

By the end of the day the ICM3 dialogue participants had captured a range of ideas on flip charts, which *idgroup* later synthesized and analyzed into a report. This report was shared with the Design Team to confirm that "we got it right." After approval, the report was handed off to the strategy team and creative team for the next step of the process—translation into an identity platform, identity narrative, strategic and tactical plan, creative assets, and customer experience initiatives.

Inspera Health's Identity Narrative

The narrative served as an expression of the identity of Inspera Health. It captures the core strengths, personality, differentiation, and brand promise, as well as the aspirations of the organization. The Inspera Health leadership team used the narrative to develop customer experience standards that ensured the words were lived throughout the organization, while the idgroup team translated it into creative assets designed to tell an authentic and inspiring story to the marketplace (see pages 268–270).

Every single day, we make choices. Choices that may affect us for a moment, or for a lifetime. Choices that stem from our behaviors and our mindsets. Choices that can have the power to change our world, and the worlds of others. Although the concepts of health and wellness are intricately linked, they aren't synonymous. Health isn't always a choice—living with multiple chronic health conditions and the complexities that accompany them isn't something anyone would choose. But we're of the mind that people can choose wellness. To look beyond the conditions that may obstruct vitality and productivity and be inspired to live a healthier, happier life, no matter the circumstances. To make a conscious decision to be well in the body and in the mind, through deliberate effort and determination. Wellness that, when practiced continuously and with resolve, results in a healthier person. We're committed to changing the lives of people living with multiple chronic health conditions by transforming those individuals into healthier and happier members of society, and in turn, improving the existence of the self-insured businesses that employ them. We are a compassionate, multi-disciplinary team, and through our intrinsic whole-person approach, we provide people with the tools to foster an internal capacity for change by inspiring hope and igniting transformation from within. We are proven successful because of our experience, skills, and track record. Despite the obvious financial parameters of the bottom line, we factor in the overall happiness and well-being of employees and ultimately, employers. Guided by research, we provide—and learn from—measurable results.

The Importance of Authenticity
By Lee Murphy, CEO
Inspera Health

We're in the business of helping people with multiple chronic conditions improve their health and their lifestyle. The people that we work with come into our program highly skeptical and highly vulnerable. When they reach our door, they've often been beaten up and feel defeated. They still have some hope, but they don't come in excited. If our team doesn't believe in what we do, our chances for success would diminish significantly. For lack of a better way to explain it, if we really believe in what we do, the vibration in the room is the vibration of authenticity, the vibration of *I care for you, I am here to help you get better*. That's how we break through the skepticism. So, the word authenticity really resonates with us.

After 21 years in business, while we're doing a lot of things well, we kept hearing "you guys are great but no one really understands your name," which at the time was Integrated Case Management L3C or ICM3. But we knew any rebranding we did had to be about something more than just looking attractive and sounding good. The Branding from the Core process resonated with us because it's all about authenticity. It's really focused on getting all of our stakeholders together and building our new brand from their stories about why we mattered to them. It all started from the inside.

We ended up with a great name and a more powerful story. But the process did more. It reinforced relationships. It helped people in our organization connect better with who we are, what we do and what we believe. Having a consistent and authentic story positioned us to be able to go out and explain who we are better, but it also created a loop that is incredibly self-reinforcing. With the good branding package and the right branding we now have the opportunity to reinforce our culture internally, for both current and prospective staff members.

Branding can be a force for attracting customers but at the end of the day, it's only a force if it reflects the truth of purpose. A purpose tied to service that is delivered and is best in class. Only then does branding make a difference. Branding from the Core was powerful because it provided the story for our team to rally around, to believe in and live up to through the way we serve our clients.

ABOUT

Lee Murphy

Lee Murphy is the CEO of Inspera Health, a social entrepreneurial venture dedicated to improving the health of patients with multiple chronic health conditions by supporting lifestyle change through integrating the physical, mental, social, spiritual, and financial aspects of life. Lee has spent his professional career in employee benefits and building businesses focused on improving the health and lifestyles of those with multiple chronic conditions. Lee can bring a focus that simultaneously values the human side of change and the reality of organizational profitability.

Mr. Murphy holds a Ph.D in Values-Based Leadership. He has a Bachelor of Science degree in Accounting and is a Certified Public Accountant (CPA). He also holds a Master of Business Administration and a Master of Science in Management and Organizational Behavior.

LEE MURPHY OPENING ADDRESS FOR BRAND ROLLOUT CELELBRATION

Healthy employees. Healthy business.

Lotus
Purity
Enlightenment
Blossoming

+

Humanity
People
Emergence
Revival

=

Balance
A combination
of balance and
celebration of life

LOGO FORMULA

> *I wanted to feel comfortable in my own skin.*
> *Now, I do.*

A different kind of health
improvement company.
insperahealth.com

inspera health

" I wanted to go on long walks with my wife
without being exhausted.
Now, I can. "

A different kind of health
improvement company.
insperahealth.com

BEYOND SIZZLE: THE NEXT EVOLUTION OF BRANDING

Final Thoughts on Branding from the Core

The strategic plan produced by your Brand Transformation Journey is your blueprint for aligning the various components of your brand ecosystem to ensure consistency between what is promised (expectations) and what is delivered (experiences). This stakeholder engagement approach to building brands on the platform of people, purpose, and performance enables your organization to engage with a growing group of potential customers and employees. These stakeholders expect your organization to deliver value, defined by the quality of its products or services and its acceptance of responsibility for making the world better.

Keeping the strategy produced through Branding from the Core at the forefront of your organization's focus and commitment will pay dividends through the development of a brand and a reputation that matters—because your organization is trusted and respected.

Every author brings perspectives of how the world works to her writing. Here are three insights into "the world according to Mona."

1. Organizations are human systems. The order of these words is important to me. Human first. Systems second. Organizations consist of people, all of whom bring their individual hopes, fears, dreams, challenges, and desires to work. The purpose of the system is to bring these humans together through structure and process to accomplish a common goal.

Purpose is the motivation that drives people to accomplish a goal. A system without a purpose is like a ship without a rudder. It will circle aimlessly with little or no forward momentum.

2. The prosperity of all organizations is dependent upon the ability of leaders to rally people around a common purpose. Purpose trumps the multiple challenges inherent in "group work." The energy binding people to a shared purpose transcends race, gender, socio-economics, intellect, skill, and any of the other external labels we use in our attempts to classify the right mix of factors that predict success. Give people a big enough reason to make something happen, and they will usually find a way to organize themselves to get it done. I am not proposing that systems, processes, and structures aren't important factors of success, however, commitment to a shared and meaningful goal is a required starting point for maximizing the potential of any organization.

3. The final underpinning of Branding from the Core is my belief in the power of stories. Stories are the glue that connects us, inspires us, and motivates us. Our need to share and hear them is baked into our DNA. Since humans first walked this earth, we have used stories to construct meaning and to share this interpretation of our reality with those around us. We use stories to help our children understand the roots of who they are, we tell stories to ourselves and others as motivation for success or encouragement when things get tough. In many

ways our reality, what we believe to be true, is constructed by the stories that we choose to connect with as part of our own evolving personal story that we call—our lives. In organizations, stories are equally important as a means to engage people in collective purpose that transcends the "what" of their work to the deeper reasons of "why" what they do matters.

As I stated earlier, organizations are unique and unfolding stories. In the final chapter of this book, the Epilogue, we return to the story of Interface as an example of an organization that has evolved to what researchers Goggins and Mirvis refer to as transformational stage of corporate citizenship (as referenced in Chapter 3). Through an interview with Erin Meezan, Executive Vice President of Sustainability at Interface, we learn more about how the organization is using its voice and influence to advocate for the values central to the company's culture through its new mission—Climate Take Back.

You say you want a revolution
Well, you know
We all want to change the world

You say you got a real solution
Well, you know
We'd all love to see the plan

— John Lennon / Paul McCartney

EPILOGUE
STILL LEARNING FROM INTERFACE

As I approached the church, the cars streaming into the parking lot reflected the number of people who had been touched by Ray's life. As I exited my car, I glanced at familiar faces as they passed, acknowledging their presence but avoiding conversation. I left very early that morning for the drive from Pensacola, Florida, to Atlanta to ensure that I arrived in time for the 11 a.m. service.

A couple days earlier, at 4:42 on a Monday afternoon, I received an email that I had expected but hoped wouldn't come. The subject line read, "Ray C Anderson 1934–2011." The email from Dan Hendrix, CEO of Interface, began: "It is with a heavy heart that I am writing to let you know that our beloved founder and chairman passed away today. He was at his home, surrounded by family and friends. Ray waged an epic battle against cancer that reflected his strong spirit and his tenacity..."

As I took my seat in the pew, my thoughts wandered to the many conversations Ray and I had over the years. Like a familiar movie soundtrack, the words began to replay in my mind, pausing on a quote he shared during one of my first interviews with him:

"If not us, who? If not now, when?"

IF NOT US, WHO? IF NOT NOW, WHEN?

With the death of Ray Anderson, the person many would describe as the engine of the Interface sustainability journey, the inescapable question became the elephant in the room: Would Interface carry on its climb up Mt. Sustainability without him? Or would what had become known as Mission Zero fade into the distance, as the company's natural life cycle inevitably brought a new generation of people who had never met Ray into the organization?

The research that I shared in the opening pages of this book concluded that, between 1994 and 2004, Interface had undergone deep culture change that had embedded the values of sustainability into the DNA of the organization. With Ray's passing, I decided to circle back to the organization to determine whether my conclusions were correct—and, perhaps, to finally answer a question that I had been asked on multiple occasions over the years: What if we don't have a Ray Anderson? Can we do this? Underlying this question was something bigger.

Was it the purpose that drove the change at Interface or the person? If that person was no longer there, would the purpose remain central to how Interface defined itself?

In this epilogue, we return to the Interface story with a conversation with Erin Meezan, Chief Sustainability Officer at Interface. Erin and I talked about the years since Ray's death and how the organization has answered these questions. Interface has gone beyond just keeping the spirit of Mission Zero alive—it has used that spirit as a platform for launching a bigger, bolder mission and purpose for the organization. The first steps of this second leg of the Interface journey were actually taken a couple months before Ray's death.

Early in 2011, Erin Meezan, along with CEO Dan Hendrix and other members of the leadership team, faced a hard question: Are we going to reach our 2020 goals? What had been a distant horizon when articulated in 1994 was now staring

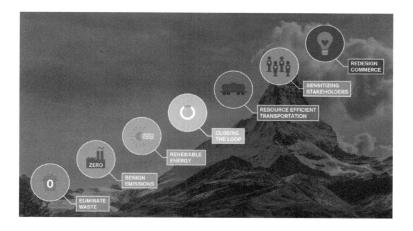

Figure 9.1. 7 Faces Of Mt. Sustainabilty—Steps To Reach Mission Zero

them in the eye. They now faced a harsh reality: They had a short nine years to reach the goals they had proclaimed to the world. Coming face to face with this truth propelled actions between

FIGURE 9.1 – 9.8 ARE PRINTED WITH PERMISSION FROM INTERFACE, INC.

2011 and 2017 that created a clear path to 2020 and beyond. This leg of the Interface Journey is reflective of the final stage of Branding from the Core: Evolution. When we revisit the Stages of Corporate Citizenship (Figure 2.2) first introduced in Chapter 2, we can see that this ongoing evolution represents the fifth and final stage of corporate responsibility. Here's the story about how Interface did it.

ABOUT

Erin Meezan

As Chief Sustainability Officer, Erin gives voice to Interface's conscience, ensuring that strategy and goals are in sync with its aggressive sustainability vision established more than 20 years ago. Today, Interface has evolved its thinking to go beyond doing less harm to creating positive impacts, not just for Interface and the flooring industry, but for the world at large.

Erin led the company to unveil a new mission in 2016 — Climate Take Back, tackling the single biggest threat facing humanity: global climate change. This mission is focused on creating a path for Interface and others to reverse global warming, not just reduce carbon emissions.

The 2011 Global Innovation Summit

There was a fear in 2011 among the people at Interface that they weren't going to make it. Innovation had slowed. While they had made some minor advances, they weren't seeing big leaps. So, the Innovation Summit was convened to kick-start thinking and to get energy refocused on figuring out how this global company was going to achieve Mission Zero. My colleague Keith Cox and I worked closely with Erin and her team, using much of the thinking outlined in the Branding from the Core methodology, to design these sessions and afterward to support the work groups' continuous learning. Our focus was on helping Interface understand what it was doing well around the world but also what needed to change to ignite innovation. The three days of meetings included the executive team and innovation teams, operations leadership and regional business unit leadership team representatives from the various global businesses, members of the Eco Dream Team, and several speakers specially chosen to shake up thinking. And even though he was fighting cancer at the time, Ray attended one of the sessions.

> *ERIN: I think we realized we had to do something, but until we had that meeting in 2011, we didn't even realize we had structural issues that were getting in our way. Interface had always been this collection of three geographical regions. When we started the sustainability focus, it became a unifying force in a company that wasn't really unified. So, other than sustainability we were pretty disconnected. We walked away from that meeting with some actionable plans for what we*

needed to do around global collaboration and communication to spur the new levels of innovation needed to reach our 2020 goals.

DEATH AND AWAKENING

In August 2011, not long after the Innovation Summit, Ray Anderson died.

ERIN: I think we just stopped for about six months. I don't know how else to describe it. It was just a strange time at the company. I think it was like those old cartoons where the guy comes in and he punches the clock and he just goes to his desk. There was certainly a huge sense of loss. Other people coming into the organization either at that time or shortly thereafter described the company as being in mourning.

We kept moving, but I do think there was just such a feeling of loss. We made some advances structurally. We went into this period for two or three years when we were quite aggressive. We implemented what we learned from our work during and after the Innovation Summit through models of co-innovation and collaboration that were born at the summit. So I think we did a really good job pushing forward some very good initiatives. For example, NetWorks, our first internal collab platform LOOP (on a JIVE technology) was launched. The naming of a global head of innovation, Nigel Stansfield, now our EMEA CEO, came out of that meeting, and the work that he did to align our operations teams in the business had a real impact on accelerating internal supply chain innovation. We set some global priorities around sustainability, supported by the executive team, that we had never done before. We saw results as innovation did move forward. Our CEO, Dan Hendrix, was doing other things to globalize the business. He put into place a chief marketing officer, and he elevated a person in the company to be a chief design officer, which was something we had never had before on the senior team. He increased his communications by putting into place some new communication tools, including "Five Minutes with Dan" and town hall meetings.

One of the conversations that happened a couple months after Ray died occurred when our CEO came to me in 2011 and said, "Are you sure that we're doing everything we can to make sure that, now that Ray is gone, we keep this culture connected to our purpose?" The question was, Are we doing enough? but what he was really asking was, Should we be doing more?

MONA: *Was there a fear inside the organization that perhaps Ray was necessary to hold this culture together, and now that he was gone, it would all just go away? Was there that level of concern?*

ERIN: No, I don't think it was "oh god, it's all going to vanish now that Ray is gone." Our CEO said at the time, "I don't doubt this is deeply embedded, but I want to know how deeply. I want to know what else I should be doing to make sure that this commitment doesn't diminish on my watch." I think he had this desire for immediate activity.

My reaction to his question was that we should learn what we were doing well before we started designing anything else. Our discussions led him to give me permission in 2012 to take a documentary film crew to most of our factories around the world to ask our employees, What does sustainability mean to you, and why does this purpose (Mission Zero) resonate with you?

The idea was to provide a quantitative and qualitative look at the programs, activities, actions, and attitudes in each region's business and try to figure out what connected people to our Mission Zero purpose. At the end of the process, we would have a report and some documentary footage that would reflect,

in our employees' own words, why they connected with Mission Zero. So we went around the world to ask our employees, What does Mission Zero mean to you?—not looking for a right or wrong answer but just their perspective about the meaning of sustainability. Most said it's something we are doing in the company to make sure that we don't harm the environment. Then, someone would go on to explain, "And in my group, it means that we are doing recycled backing." So what was amazing is that people could articulate the big picture, but they could translate it to how they were a part of that bigger purpose. For example, if I talked to a janitor in Australia, he could tell me, "We're trying to have zero footprint, but that means that I make sure that we don't throw things away." Really powerful. We didn't talk about Ray. I don't think we even asked people about Ray. I think we did that very purposefully.

The video really gave people such an amazing gift. When I showed those videos to our senior team, and I shared the report that said that within ten minutes of walking into any of our factories, it was clear that people got the mission, and they were connected to it and how it related to their job. An interesting added surprise is that they [the employees] talked about how it had also changed the way they thought about the world.

If anyone in the organization had lingering fears that this would all go away because Ray was gone, and maybe Dan (CEO) secretly had some concern, I think this took any fear away. It confirmed, Mona, what your research told us—Interface was a company with these values really, really deeply embedded in our culture, beyond Ray.

MONA: Why do you think this resonated so strongly with people from LaGrange, Georgia, to Halifax to São Paulo and beyond?

ERIN: I think it's about people's innate desire to be a part of something bigger. When you offer them something bigger—in

this instance, to have your work have a context that's a little more meaningful than just making the product—I think there's something innate in humans that allows us all to connect into that.

Our mission offers the opportunity for people to participate in something meaningful—which humans really want. As an organization, we allowed regionalization—that is, we allowed each location to enter into our bigger purpose in a way that was culturally significant for them. What we smartly didn't do is say, "Mission Zero is about putting this bit in the recycling bin." Rather, we said, "It's about getting to this broad goal (sustainability), and there are many different ways to do that." How will you be a part of this?

NEW LEADERSHIP

In 2015, a new COO, Jay D. Gould, was brought into the organization from outside the company and tapped to be the next CEO of Interface. But the decision was made that he would work inside the company for a couple years as COO to make sure that he was a fit with the company's culture before elevating him to the top office.

After the 2012 documentary project, there was confidence that Mission Zero was firmly planted in the values of the organization. So, Interface pushed on. But internal conversations intensified about not just reaching 2020, but about what the next mountain the company would climb might be.

ERIN: Those who had been associated with Ray Anderson felt a deep obligation to see the mission through. People began to add as part of our internal dialogue, "We have to get to 2020"—then they would add, "for Ray." He would never have liked that when he was around, but this was an interesting thing that happened after he died. We all seemed to want to remind ourselves that we had this extra obligation now.

At the same time, we had loads of new people coming into the organization who had never interacted with Ray. So after his death, I think it became obvious that this wasn't just about keeping the flame going; it was about igniting new flames.

It was really gratifying that when Jay [COO] came in, the top of his agenda was figuring out a clear map to 2020. He immediately saw that there wasn't a clear plan. He saw the disconnectedness and I think it concerned him. He asked our executive team to figure out what the five things were that we were going to do to get to 2020 and how we were going to pay for it. He said, "We are all going to commit to this. We're going to get to 2020 for Ray." Then he added, "You have permission to go build the next map. Come back to the executive team with how we're going to achieve Mission Zero; then we're going to name a new mission." What emerged from that assignment was the level of detail that we needed to map our next steps. So I think that what was great about getting permission to build the map to 2020 and what's next is that it erased any doubts that people at all levels of the organization may have had about a new leader coming in—that we were still going to be Interface and that we were still going to get to 2020.

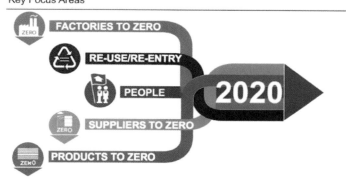

Path to 2020
Key Focus Areas

FACTORIES TO ZERO

RE-USE/RE-ENTRY

PEOPLE

2020

SUPPLIERS TO ZERO

PRODUCTS TO ZERO

Figure 9.2. System Thinking Used by Interface

Figure 9.2 provides a picture of how Interface used system thinking to define key platforms to drive the organization to 2020:

1. *Factories to Zero:* tackles factory waste, water usage, energy efficiency, and renewable energy.

2. *Re-use/Re-entry:* capabilities that provide closed-loop recycling.

3. *People:* ambassadors engage even more with employees to influence and support this incredible journey.

4. *Suppliers to Zero:* helps the supply chain become more sustainable.

5. *Products to Zero:* focuses on the carbon footprint and chemistry of the products (designing products with bio-based raw materials that were more recyclable).

I think it's important to clarify that in 2016 this provided a snapshot and a roadmap of what's left to do to hit our 2020 targets. In years past we had the seven fronts that focused on waste, energy, etc. This took what gaps we saw from the original seven fronts framework and put them into clear workstreams where we not only looked at what we had done, but what gaps we had left to meet, and we mapped out the initiatives under each one of these pathways to see how far we could get. Then we projected the success we thought we could get to by 2020 (see Figure 9.3). But since then, we've adjusted our numbers and projections. The projections will change every year—this is an ongoing conversation we will have in the lead up to 2020 and beyond.

Mission Zero Progress 2017 and Projected 2020 Progress

GREEN numbers indicate improvement over prior year.	NOW		2020
ENERGY USE	▼	43%	▼ 50%
RENEWABLE ENERGY	▲	88%	▲ 90%
GHG EMISSIONS	▼	96%	▼ 96%
WASTE TO LANDFILL	▼	91%	▼ 100%
WATER INTAKE	▼	88%	▼ 90%
RECYCLED & BIOBASED MATERIALS USED[1]	▲	61%	▲ 91%
PRODUCT CARBON FOOTPRINT	▼	66%	▼ 80%

[1]Recycled & Biobased Materials = 58% of Sales including LVT

Figure 9.3. Projections for Mission Zero Progress

Beyond 2020

Dan Hendrix officially retired as CEO of Interface and became chairman of the board in 2017, and Jay Gould stepped up to be the new CEO. He's only the third person to hold that position since the company's founding in 1973, and the first person hired from outside the organization. With a new CEO in place, and a clear map to 2020 designed, the leadership team turned its attention to shaping a new mission beyond 2020. The result moved Interface's focus beyond doing no harm (Mission Zero) to doing more good. What had taken Interface several years to figure out (by 1994 when they chartered Mission Zero), was now accomplished in twelve months. The result is a three-pronged strategy to achieve Interface's new mission, dubbed Climate Take Back.

> ERIN: The sustainability team had come up with a process that included an intensive round of surveys and opinion-gathering, asking people who they wanted to be in the future and how we should name that and what issues they thought were important. We had a sense that the idea of sustainability within our company had already shifted from do no harm to do more good, and we wanted a ratification of that. But at that point, there was an interesting point of tension with our new CEO, who wanted to hire an outside agency to write the new mission—frame it and brand it. My team strongly defended our approach, which we felt was truer to our company's culture. We ended up with a compromise that respected both Jay's goals and our process.
>
> At the time, the CEO had also undertaken a parallel process to define and summarize the organization's values and purpose that culminated in the articulation of a set of values, a new purpose statement (Lead industry to love the world),

and a celebration video—none of this process influenced our content or our process, but I think the combo of the two parallel processes did have a combined effect to reignite some interest and excitement. And, of course, we rolled them out together as a package—values that reinforced who we were, the new purpose statement, the video, the five pathways to Mission Zero, and the new mission (an articulation of the carbon mission). We had two work streams (and as much as I resisted the outside agency owning all of this, their work on the values, the purpose statement, and the film really complemented our internal process around the Beyond 2020 internal feedback and new mission articulation.

DESIGNING INTERFACE'S FUTURE TOGETHER

The process used by Erin and her team to shape the next Interface mission reflected a deep understanding of the company's culture. From the early days of the sustainability journey, the people of Interface had been tasked with charting the course up Mt. Sustainability; now they were being asked to lend their voices to answering the question, What's next? This was perhaps the single most important step the company took to ensure that the values that had defined Interface since 1994 remained at the core of the company's culture.

ERIN: Our approach for shaping the next mission included an internal deep-dive based on the work and process we had done with you, Mona, during the 2011 Innovation Summit. We shared with Jay that we firmly believed that "the answers are in the room, and our people can write this." With his blessing, we moved forward with surveys of people from every corner of our business. Based on what we learned, our sustainability team, and in some instances our people, sat down with five to ten of their coworkers and walked them through a conversation that talked about the future and where they wanted the company to go.

We then took what we learned to an Eco Dream Team meeting with some external advisors, then a senior leadership deep-dive. From there we shaped the details of our new mission—which coalesces around the idea of climate change.

FROM SKEPTICISM TO COMMITMENT

When the discussion about climate change focused on Interface's next mission, there was some pushback from the executive team, who claimed that the company was too small to influence climate change.

ERIN: I think that what we were seeing was a lack of belief that we could really do something meaningful as a business. Basically, they were saying that we shouldn't engage in this conversation because we couldn't fix it. After a lot of conversations, and inspiration from the Eco Dream Team, we ultimately decided that we wanted to frame the new mission around climate—we named it Climate Take Back. But we wanted to look at the issue differently from anyone else. Most companies are focused on setting goals around climate that are way too small to be meaningful, and they're all focused on reducing carbon emissions. We challenged ourselves to set a much more ambitious goal—reversing. Our ambition was to aim for a mission focused on reversing global warming, and the challenge we now have is to build a plan for the company that focuses on reversal, one that not just reduces carbon but removes it and utilizes it.

Mission Zero stayed Mission Zero. By design we built Mission Zero into Climate Take Back—we made it the foundation.

Because zero footprint as a business has become part of how we do business, it made sense to always preserve that mindset and link to our past, but by naming Live Zero as the first part of the new mission's framework, we are acknowledging that we must continue to love this, to make it part of our daily approach. The language has become embedded in the organization—that's what people call it. It remains an aggressive goal to have zero footprint and impact as a business. We have said to people that this has become our business as usual. Live Zero-Mission Zero, will become just how we do business. Now it's time to step it up. I think that served to offset another anxiety in the organization, which was people on my team and others in the organization saying that the world's changing—the definition of what it means to be a sustainable business has evolved from a reduce-your-footprint mindset, and our thinking about our plan and approach needed to evolve too. I think, as a result of this evolution, that we were seeing that Mission Zero was not as exciting as it was twenty-four years ago. So I think that if we had just come back to the organization and said that we're still getting to Mission Zero for Ray, and we had not articulated anything beyond that, the level of excitement or buy-in would not have been as high as it is now. What we did by framing the next step is to give a lot more energy and excitement behind Mission Zero.

So now we've taken a step that's so important to preserving Ray's legacy. And in the process, we've maintained the culture that he wanted to have and that he created.

I am optimistic and hopeful that other people can do what we've done because we've shown that we created that connection to sustainability in parts of the world where they never interacted with Ray. If you look at the progress we made in those factories in Europe, for example, it's significant. They are connected to it emotionally. And this is not because they knew Ray, not because they saw him, not because they had the experience I had with him where I saw him give the speech

> *fifty times and felt very emotionally connected to him as an individual in addition to the mission—they just felt connected to the mission.*

So let's return to the question that opened this chapter, Was it the purpose or the person that propelled Interface to embrace the mission of sustainability? While we all agree that Ray was a powerful source of inspiration and an unyielding crusader for the environmental and social responsibility of business, it's abundantly clear that the purpose embraced by the company reached beyond a single person.

The seed of possibility that was planted by Ray Anderson continues to be nurtured by a new generation of Interface leaders and employees who are bold enough to embrace the belief that they (and Interface) can leave the world better— because they were here.

Climate Take Back (Interface 2018)

"IF HUMANITY HAS CHANGED THE CLIMATE BY MISTAKE, CAN WE CHANGE IT WITH INTENT?" — INTERFACE.COM

At Interface, we're convinced a fundamental change needs to happen in our global response to climate change. We need to stop just thinking about how to limit the damage caused by climate change and start thinking about how to create a climate fit for life.

After decades of hard work, Interface is poised to reach our Mission Zero® goals by 2020.

Climate Take Back™ is our new mission and we want to share it with the world. We commit to running our business in a way that creates a climate fit for life—and we call on others to do the same.

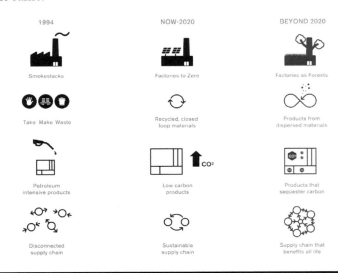

Figure 9.4

Figure 9.4. Going from doing less harm to doing more good. While all of these new goals address carbon, the technology involved in drawing down carbon has other positive benefits as well.

Figure 9.5. Imagine a new set of metrics for factory performance that create positive impact and pull down carbon.

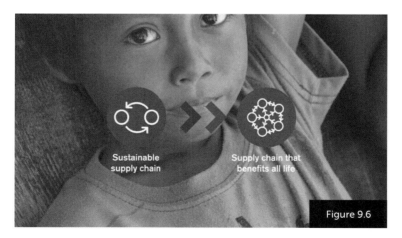

Figure 9.6. Going from a supply chain that does no harm to one that enriches many by influencing our suppliers to change how

they think about their role. This includes working on our specific sourcing agreements to make sure that we are benefiting others.

Figure 9.7. (Ray C. Anderson) We are calling for a new level of desired impact, not just for Interface but increasingly for more stakeholder groups.

Figure 9.8. Mission Zero was set by Ray but done by us—this next mission is created by us for all of us.

IF HUMANITY
HAS CHANGED
THE CLIMATE
BY MISTAKE,

CAN WE
CHANGE IT
WITH INTENT?

Every Ending Offers A New Beginning

It has been almost twenty-five years since Ray first challenged his global carpet manufacturing company to become the "first name in industrial sustainability in deeds, not just words." He felt an ethical pull to do the right thing, but he also saw that proving that his company could be an exemplar of sustainability was also the smart thing to do. He was among one of the first leaders to embrace what today is labeled *conscious capitalism*. He sought a better way to bigger profits by asking new questions that challenged his people to transform Interface into what he defined as the prototypical company of the twenty-first century, a model that heralded the dawning of the new era of sustainable manufacturing.

Today Interface stands as a testament to the impact of visionary leadership. Ray Anderson knew there was a better way 'round the bend, and he had the courage to embark on a journey that at that point in time, few had traveled. The company's story continues to evolve as a rejection of the false choice that so many leaders feel they face—the choice between profitability and ethical responsibilities. To the contrary, seeing business through a new lens offers uplifting lessons about how stepping up to meaningful, yet seemingly impossible, challenges can take organizations to new levels of performance. New solutions emerge when people are challenged to see the world differently, particularly when the answers have impact beyond the moment. Magic happens when the hearts of customers, employees, and other stakeholders are engaged in a journey of purpose.

Climate Take Back is the next big challenge the people of Interface have embraced. They are determined to demonstrate the potential of business to reach beyond a commitment to doing no harm to actually becoming an active force for doing good. They are facing challenges by asking new questions that are anchored in hope and possibility, not in the doom and gloom usually associated with the issue of climate change. They're not sure how they'll get there, but they're confident that they'll figure it out. Once again, the company is embarking on a new journey to the unknown and people want to be part of it.

The mantra of successful business is to give customers what they want, or they will likely go away. As the demand grows for business to demonstrate value beyond profitability, leaders will continue to be challenged to respond to the growing call for organizations to prove their commitment to the values of social and environmental responsibility. Embracing this responsibility to be good citizens is likely to define the difference between simply surviving, and thriving.

While the Interface journey served as the launching point for the ideas in this book, every company must discover its own answers and set its own course to becoming a brand that matters to their customers, employees, and the world. *Beyond Sizzle* responds to those ready for this journey by offering Branding from the Core as a map that reaches beyond philosophical hopes to provide an actionable process that will unleash the potential for people to dream, to achieve, and to ultimately contribute to creating a healthier, more productive, and more prosperous organization. Part of that journey is placing the purpose at the core of who the company is.

"Hope is generated and is sustained when people, facing the mystery of the future, dialogue about their highest human ideals..."(Ludema, Wilmot, and Srivastva, 1997). This echoes the perspectives that I chose to open this book. People have the need to connect with each other and to something beyond the here and now—to actively engage in the pursuit of dreams beyond the mundane necessities of survival. This noble purpose has been identified over the centuries as a motivating force of human behavior. I hope that this book will serve as motivation for you to discover the unique legacy that you and your organization will leave to future generations. "If not us, who? If not now, when?"

"IF NOT US, WHO? IF NOT NOW, WHEN?"

"If you want to go fast, go alone.
If you want to go far, go together."

— African Proverb

Acknowledgments

The central themes throughout this book are anchored in the work of some amazing thinkers and doers I've had the opportunity to work with and learn from over the years. At the head of the list is Dr. Mary Jo Hatch, who, with her research partner Dr. Majken Schultz, created Identity Dynamics, which is the foundational theory for much of the thinking shared in this book. But more than just a scholar, Mary Jo has offered many years of advice, friendship, and encouragement to me. Her support, together with that of Ray Anderson, gave me hope that maybe I had something important to say.

Thank you, to Jim Hartzfeld, former Vice President of Sustainable Strategy with Interface, for setting up that first interview with Ray Anderson and for being my thinking partner as I discovered the answers to the questions that motivated my research with Interface.

With gratitude to Erin Meezan, Vice President and Chief Sustainability Officer at Interface, for her collaboration on the Epilogue and her generous gift of time and insights throughout the process of writing this book.

Also inspiring have been our *idgroup* clients, who have taught me so much over the years. I owe a debt of gratitude to them for trusting us and the process as we developed the ideas presented in this book.

This journey has been inspired by a host of professors—most notably Dr. Jim Ludema, Founder and Director of Benedictine University Center for Values-Driven Leadership; Dr. Ken Murrell, Professor Emeritus, University of West Florida; and Dr. Phil Mirvis, whose pioneering work on corporate citizenship was foundational in shaping the idea of organizations as brands that matter. His best advice to me about this book was "just write the damn thing." He was right. Thank you, Phil, for the loving nudge.

I offer a big thanks to my colleagues who offered comments on the manuscript though various points in development: Dr. Keith Cox, Dr. Mary Jo Hatch, Dr. Jackie Stavros, Jim Sparks, Amber Johnson, Carly Quina Ross, and members of the current *idgroup* team Gail Spruill-Shaw, Mariah Crawford, Lindsey Braxton Shook, Nick Gray, Somi Choi, Kristoffer Poore, Danielle Kelly, Erin Wachtel Stubbs, and Julie Orr.

I hold the members of the *idgroup* team, past and present, in a special place in my heart. You continue to inspire me with your passion, creativity, and commitment to the belief in the power of brands that matter to change the world—in particular, Kristoffer Poore, Vice-President and Executive Creative Director, who over the past eleven years has helped shape the Branding from the Core process. He has probably read more versions of this book than anyone. Thank you, Kris, for keeping the faith. It is fitting that Kris created the cover design for this book and worked closely with me in writing the Branding from the Core Playbook in Part II. Thanks to Lindsey Braxton Shook, Vice-President Operations and Director of Client Services, for keeping the wheels on the bus at *idgroup*, which allowed me the time to complete this book. And, finally, I give a huge thank you to Somi Choi, *idgroup's* lead designer, for her patience with my many changes as we worked through the design of this book. Thank you to Tika Gulick for the final proofreading of the manuscript. Tika was *idgroup's* first production manager, so it was particularly meaningful for me to have her involved with this project.

Thank you to Andrea Barilla, who served as the early development editor. I offer my appreciation to her for helping me shape my often-fuzzy sentences into what I wanted to say. My deep appreciation goes to Jim Pennypacker, Publisher of Maven House Press, for taking a chance on this first-time author. Everyone needs someone who believes they can do it. Thank you, Jim, for believing in this project and in me.

No one writes a book without the support of friends and family. I am fortunate to have an abundance of both who have encouraged me throughout this process. I offer my love and gratitude to each of them. I want to offer a smile of appreciation to Julie Sheppard, Randy Hammer, Teresa Dos Santos, and Jill Thomas for the "wineversations," that played an important part in this process. To Dr. Martha D. Saunders, President of the University of West Florida, who is not only my friend but an inspirational leader who has taught me so much about walking the talk of authentic, purposeful leadership—thank you for being there for me.

In closing, thanks to my brother and sister, Anthony Amodeo and Lisa Amodeo, for your phone calls of support. Yes, it's finished. Beau and Chew, my four-legged writing partners who were always there with me during those 4:30 a.m. writing sessions. They now know more about branding and culture change than most humans.

A big hug and thank you to my husband, Ken, who has never wavered in his willingness to listen to just one more idea or to read one more "final" draft. He is very happy this book is finished.

And finally, to Carter Braxton Shook, my grandson—thank you for your smile that always reminds me what's right with the world.

THE END

MONA A. AMODEO
Gulf Breeze, Florida
June 1, 2018

References

Albert, Stuart, and David A. Whetten. 1985. "Organizational Identity." *Research in Organizational Behavior* 7: 263–95.

Amodeo, Mona 2008. "The Interface Journey to Sustainability." In *Sustainable Work Systems* (2nd edition), edited by Peter Docherty, Miri Kira, and A. B. (Rami) Shani. London: Routledge Press.

Bernays, Edward L. 1928. *Propaganda*. United Kingdom: Routledge.

B Lab. 2017. "846 Companies Honored as Best for the World, Creating Positive Impact for Workers, Environment, Community." CSRwire, September 12. Accessed March 23, 2018, http://www.csrwire.com/press_releases/40349-846-Companies-Honored-as-Best-for-the-World-Creating-Positive-Impact-for-Workers-Environment-Community.

B Lab. 2018. "Conscious Company Magazine." Accessed on March 23, 2018, https://www.bcorporation.net/community/conscious-company-magazine.

Barrett, Richard. 2018. "Levels of Leadership Consciousness." Barrett Values Centre. Accessed April 20, 2018, https://www.valuescentre.com/mapping-values/barrett-model/leadership-consciousness.

Cameron, Kim S., Jane E. Dutton, and Robert E. Quinn, editors. 2003. *Positive Organizational Scholarship: Foundations of a New Discipline*. Oakland, CA: Berrett-Koehler.

Cooperrider, David L., and Suresh Srivastva. 1987. "Appreciative Inquiry in Organizational Life." In *Research in Organizational Change and Development, Vol. 1,* edited by Richard W. Woodman and William A. Pasmore, 129–69. Stamford, CT: JAI Press.

Davis, Ian. 2005. "The Biggest Contract." *The Economist*, May 25.

Deloitte. 2017. "Apprehensive Millennials: Seeking Stability and Opportunities in an Uncertain World." *The 2017 Deloitte Millennial Survey.*

Denhardt, R. B. 1987. "Images of Death and Slavery in Organizational Life. *Journal of Management* 13, 529–41.

Dimock, Michael. 2018. "Defining Generations: Where Millennials End and Post-Millennials Begin." Pew Research Center. Accessed April 30, 2018, http://www.pewresearch.org/fact-tank/2018/03/01/defining-generations-where-millennials-end-and-post-millennials-begin/.

Edelman. 2017. "Edelman Trust Barometer." Accessed March 15, 2017, https://www.edelman.com/trust2017/.

Feldmeth, Josh. 2016. "The Alpha of Cohesiveness." Interbrand. Accessed April 30, 2018, http://interbrand.com/best-brands/best-global-brands/2016/articles/the-alpha-of-cohesiveness/.

Fortune. 2018. "100 Best Companies to Work For." Accessed April 30, 2018, http://fortune.com/best-companies/.

Fox, A. 1980. "The Meaning of Work." In *The Politics of Work and Occupations*, edited by Geoff Esland and Graeme Salaman. Toronto: University of Toronto Press.

Frampton, Jez. 2018. "Growth in a Changing World." *Best Global Brands 2017*. Interbrand. Accessed April 30, 2018, http://interbrand.com/best-brands/best-global-brands/2017/articles/growth-in-a-changing-world/.

Gidman, Jenn. 2017. "Patagonia Owner Sues Over Bears Ears: I Won't Let 'Evil' Win." *Newser*, December 7. Accessed April 30, 2018, http://www.newser.com/story/252557/patagonia-owner-sues-over-bears-ears-i-wont-let-evil-win.html.

GlobeScan. 2017. *The GlobeScan-SustainAbility Survey: The 2017 Sustainability Leaders*. GlobeScan.

Godin, Seth. 2008. *Tribes: We Need You to Lead Us*. New York: Portfolio.

Googins, Bradley K., Philip K. Mirvis, and Steven A. Rochlin. 2007. *Beyond Good Company: The Next Generation of Corporate Citizens*. New York: Palgrave MacMillan.

Groysberg, Boris, Jeremiah Lee, Jesse Price, and J. Yo-Jud Cheng. 2018. "The Leader's Guide to Corporate Culture." *Harvard Business Review*, January.

Hatch, Mary Jo, and Majken Schultz. 2001. "Are the Strategic Stars Aligned for Your Corporate Brand?" *Harvard Business Review*, February.

Hatch, Mary Jo, and Majken Schultz. 2002. "The Dynamics of Organizational Identity." *Human Relations 55*, no. 8 (August 1): 989–1018.

Hatch, Mary Jo, Majken Schultz, and Mogens Holten Larsen. 2000. *The Expressive Organization: Linking Identity, Reputation, and the Corporate Brands*. Oxford, UK: Oxford University Press.

Interface. 2018. "Climate Take Back." Accessed April 30, 2018, http://www.interface.com/US/en-US/campaign/climate-take-back/Climate-Take-Back.

Johnson, Caitlin. 2006. "Cutting Through Advertising Clutter." *CBS Sunday Morning*, September 17. Accessed April 30, 2018, https://www.cbsnews.com/news/cutting-through-advertising-clutter/.

Katz, Daniel, and Robert L. Kahn. 1966. *The Social Psychology of Organization*. New York: John Wiley & Sons.

Katz, Daniel, and Robert L. Kahn. 1978. *The Social Psychology of Organization, Second Edition*. New York: John Wiley & Sons.

Kolb, David A., and Robert Fry. 1976. "Toward an Applied Theory of Experiential Learning." In *Theories of Group Processes*, edited by Cary L. Cooper. London: John Wiley & Sons.

Kuhn, Thomas. 1962. *The Structure of Scientific Revolutions*. Chicago: University of Chicago Press.

Lewin, Kurt. 1948. *Resolving Social Conflicts*. New York: Harper and Row.

Ludema, James D., David L. Cooperrider, and Frank J. Barrett. 2001. "Appreciative Inquiry: The Power of the Unconditional Positive Question." In *Handbook of Action Research:Participative Inquiry and Practice*, edited by Peter Reason and Hilary Bradbury. Thousand Oaks, CA: Sage Publications.

Ludema, James D., Timothy B. Wilmot, and Suresh Srivastva. 1997. "Organizational Hope: Reaffirming the Constructive Task of Social and Organizational Inquiry." *Human Relations* 50, no. 8 (August 1): 1015–1052.

Mackey, John, and Raj Sisodia. 2013. *Conscious Capitalism: Liberating the Heroic Spirit of Business*. Cambridge, MA: Harvard Business Review Press.

Maffesoli, Michel. 1996. *The Time of the Tribes: The Decline of Individualism in Mass Society*. Thousand Oaks, CA: Sage Publishing.

Muniz, Jr., Albert M., and Thomas C. O'Guinn. 2001. "Brand Community." *Journal of Consumer Research* 27, no. 4 (March): 412–32.

Murray, Alan. 2015. "Introducing Fortune's Change the World List." *Fortune*, August 20. Accessed April 30, 2018, http://fortune.com/2015/08/20/introducing-change-the-world-list/.

Naisbitt, John, and Patricia Aburdene. 1990. *Megatrends 2000: Ten New Directions for the 1990's*. New York: William Morrow and Company.

Neumeier, Marty. 2015. *The Brand Flip: Why Customers Now Run Companies—and How to Profit from It*. San Francisco: New Riders.

Nielsen. 2014. "Doing Well by Doing Good." *The Nielsen Global Survey of Corporate Social Responsibility*. Accessed April 30, 2018, http://www.nielsen.com/us/en/insights/reports/2014/doing-well-by-doing-good.html.

NumNum. 2018. "Bite for Bite." Accessed March 23, 2018, https://numnumbaby.us/pages/charity.

Patagonia. 2018a. "Patagonia's Mission Statement." Accessed March 23, 2018. http://www.patagonia.com/company-info.html.

Patagonia. 2018b. "Becoming a Responsible Company." Accessed March 23, 2018, http://www.patagonia.com/responsible-company.html.

Peters, Tom, and Robert H. Waterman Jr. 1982. *In Search of Excellence*. New York: Harper & Row.

Price, Michelle L. 2017. "Patagonia, Outdoor Retailers Fight Trump on U.S. Monuments." *Chicago Tribune,* December 8.

Ray, Paul, and Sherry Ruth Anderson. 2000. *The Cultural Creatives: How 50 Million People Are Changing the World.* New York: Harmony Books.

Ray, Paul. 2017. "Cultural Creatives." Accessed March 22, 2018, www. cultural creatives.org/cultural-creatives.

"Revolution: Apple Changing the World." 2018. Recode and MSNBC. April 6.

Sanchez, Mary. 2003. "Ten Ways to Be a Good Citizen." Accessed March 23, 2018, http://www.sanchezclass.com/goodcitizen.htm.

Schein, Edgar. 1985. *Organizational Culture and Leadership, First Edition.* New York: Jossey Bass Wiley.

Small Business Administration. 2017. *Frequently Asked Questions About Small Business.* U.S. Small Business Administration Office of Advocacy, August.

Statista. 2018. "Advertising spending in the world's largest ad markets in 2017 (in million U.S. dollars)." Accessed April 30, 2018, https://www.statista.com/statistics/273736/advertising-expenditure-in-the-worlds-largest-ad-markets/.

Stavros, Jacqueline M., and Gina Hinrichs. 2009. *The Thin Book of SOAR: Building Strengths-Based Strategy.* Bend, OR: Thin Book Publishing.

Tajfel, Henri, and John Turner. 1979. "An Integrative Theory of Intergroup Conflict." In *The Social Psychology of Intergroup Relations*, edited by William G. Austin and Stephen Worchel. Monterey, CA: Brooks/Cole.

Vargas, Michael. 2016. "The Next Stage of Social Entrepreneurship: Benefit Corporations and the Companies Using This Innovative Corporate Form." *Business Law Today*, July 1.

York, Peter, and Mark Damazer. 2014. "Wally Ollins Obituary." Accessed March 23, 2018, https://www.theguardian.com/media/2014/apr/15/wally-olins/.

von Bertalanffy, Ludwig. 1972. "The History and Status of General Systems Theory." *The Academy of Management Journal* 15, no. 4 (December 1972): 407–26.

Index

dialogue stage, 214
differentiated value proposition, 239
differentiation, 39
distinctiveness, 79, 211
durability, 79

E

Economist, The
    on public good, 51
ecosystem as model, 169–72
education of employees, 256
emotional associations, 92
employees
    attracting the best, 56
    and brand advocates, 81–82
    connecting, 83
    and CSR programs, 106
    educating, 256
    shaping advertising, 155
evolution and learning, 252–57
evolution stage, 215–16
execution, 247–50
execution stage, 215
expectations
    and communication, 248–49
    and experiences, 58–60
    and purpose, 40–41
    and trust, 25
experiences and expectations, 58–60

experiential learning, 252–53
external people, ideas of, 210

F

findings report, 223
first order change, 137
force field analysis, 217
Fortune magazine
    on companies doing good, 49–51

G

Gen Xers, 95
Golden Age of Advertising, 28–30, 34
good citizen, 128

H

human systems, 272–73
hyperconnectivity, 25, 35–39, 84

I

IBM's Corporate Service Corps (CSC), 106
identification, 65–68
identity
    in brand ecosystem, 58
    in relationship to others, 69–70
    and reputation, 173
identity, organization, 177–78

About the Author

Mona Amodeo, Ph.D., is an award-winning management strategist and recognized expert in organization development and change. Her work spans the boundaries of scholarship and practice in the disciplines of branding, communications, and organization culture. Through her doctoral research at the world's largest manufacturer of modular carpet, Interface Inc., Mona identified critical steps to the company's success in transforming itself from a fossil fuel-dependent business to a global leader in industrial sustainability.

Mona's research on culture change has been published in the Worldwatch Institute's *State of the World Report*, *The Appreciative Inquiry Journal*, *Practicing Organization Development*, *Creating Sustainable Work Systems*, *Beyond Good Company: The Next Generation of Corporate Citizenship*, *Research in Organization Development and Change,* and *Organization Theory: Modern, Symbolic, and Postmodern Perspectives*. She has been a guest speaker at Harvard University Executive Education for Sustainable Leadership, Benedictine University Center for Values-Driven Leadership, U.S. Green Building Council, Sustainable Brands Conference, Academy of Management, and the Center for Entrepreneurship at the University of West Florida.

In her book, *Beyond Sizzle: The Next Evolution of Branding*, Mona shares the secrets to igniting transformation by leveraging organization development principles and change management approaches as a new framework for business leaders to manage their brands.

Believing that true fulfillment is achieved at the intersection of purpose and practice, Mona founded the brand transformation firm, *idgroup*, in 1989, and, along with her team, developed the Branding from the Core® methodology as a whole system approach to transforming organizations into brands that matter to customers, employees, and the world.

FIND OUT MORE ABOUT MONA AT
monaamodeo.com

Portrait by Nick Gray

About *idgroup*

idgroup is an award-winning brand transformation firm with a fundamentally different approach to branding.

Situated on the Gulf Coast in Pensacola, Florida, and founded in 1989, *idgroup* originally began as a traditional marketing and advertising agency. Through the leadership of founder and president Mona Amodeo, *idgroup* became an early pioneer in the social responsibility movement and re-positioned itself by helping leaders and organizations of all sizes make a bigger difference for their employees, customers, and the world. This commitment to utilizing business as a force of good was further strengthened in 2018 when *idgroup* achieved Certified B Corp status.

By utilizing the Branding from the Core approach, *idgroup*—along with its transformation consultants and creative teams—helps organizations achieve new levels of prosperity through image development strategies and customer experience programs that align an organization's culture and image with its vision. In the process, *idgroup* helps leaders engage their stakeholders in telling and living an authentic brand story that achieves brand clarity and elevates their brand's value and reputation.

idgroup works with clients across multiple for-profit and non-profit industries to reimagine their organizations as brands that matter to their customers, employees, and the world.

CPSIA information can be obtained at www.ICGtesting.com
Printed in the USA
LVIW01n0850240818
587951LV00001B/1

* 9 7 8 1 9 3 8 5 4 8 1 5 4 *